CANDICE OLSON

on design

PHOTOGRAPHS BY BRANDON BARRÉ

Meredith® Books, Des Moines, Iowa

Meredith Books, 1716 Locust Street
Des Moines, Iowa 50309-3023
www.meredithbooks.com

First Edition. Printed in the United States of America.
Library of Congress Control Number: 2005929394
ISBN-13: 978-0-696-22584-0; ISBN-10: 0-696-22584-0 tradepaper; ISBN-13: 978-0-696-23235-0; ISBN-10: 0-696-23235-9 hardcover

FUSION TELEVISION INC.

To My Mom

Who single-handedly raised me with a firm but loving hand, who taught me the value of hard work and that failure only makes success taste sweeter, who gave me the knowledge to think for myself and pushed me to follow my heart and dreams, and who always supported me in my search to "find" myself.

TABLE OF CONTENTS

LIFE IS FUNNY!

ODD AS IT MAY SOUND, I LEARNED A LOT OF WHAT I KNOW ABOUT LIFE—AND MYSELF—FROM A VOLLEYBALL.

I SPENT THREE YEARS OF UNIVERSITY "FINDING" MYSELF … LEARNING ABOUT PSYCHOLOGY, BIOLOGY, KINESIOLOGY, AND CHEMISTRY. Finding myself meant learning that sciences weren't for me. Too much left-brain thinking was making my head lopsided! Finding myself also meant discovering that art, which I always excelled at, didn't have to be just a hobby. You really could have a professional, put-food-on-the-table career in the arts. Interior design was the perfect balance that bridged the technical, scientific world with the artistic, creative one. I packed my bags and headed off to earn a four-year degree in interior design and I've never looked back.

During my teenage years and into my university years, I played volleyball—not the family-picnic, neighborhood-party variety, but the training-eight-hours-a-day kind. I often played opponents who had the size and temperament of pro wrestlers who found great joy in drilling a ball off my noggin with enough G-force to render me a permanent bobble-head doll. Any sport at the elite level is cutthroat—and volleyball is no exception.

In university I learned subjects ... drawing and design basics, drafting, building and mechanical systems. I worked while going to school, so I also learned about real life—how to cram for exams and keep myself up for several nights in a row to finish design assignments—hooray for coffee! In school I gained specific knowledge that has been invaluable to me in my career, but it was a ball—specifically a volleyball—that taught me about me.

Without the countless hours of intense training, I would never have known how far I could push myself. When I thought I was at my knocked-down, dragged-out limit, I found that I could reach deep down and, with the help of persuasive coaches and teammates, pull out just a little more. In short, volleyball taught me how to work hard—really, really hard. To this day, I've never thought that I'm any more talented than the next designer—I just work harder, and hard work pays off!

Playing a team sport also taught me that you are only as successful as the rest of your team. You must respect, motivate, and believe in your team to reach any level of success. And the Interior design business is no different. I can design the most incredible spaces, but without a talented team of craftspeople and tradespeople executing my drawings, it's all for naught. I've learned that it all comes down to a mutual respect for what we all do, and my mantra is simple—I make my team look good by creating the best possible design I can, and they make me look good by executing it to the best of their ability. I love to push them with new ideas and I love it when they push me with building ideas or suggestions to better execute the design. This is not a business for egos! When a project is successfully completed, we all feel a huge sense of accomplishment.

BELOW Age 16, and a member of our high school provincial championship

Volleyball also taught me about healthy competitiveness, about strategizing and executing a plan, and about the value of defeat—you only can understand how great success is if you've tasted failure. I don't want to take away from all of the teachers and professors who taught me over the years, but I do owe a lot to a simple, white, topstitched leather ball.

LIFE IS FUNNY—WE SPEND SO MUCH OF OUR LIVES WANTING WHAT OTHER PEOPLE HAVE. Our family has thin, straight hair. I mean, poker straight. I don't think we've seen a wave or a curl in the family in six generations! As a kid, I was obsessed with having a head full of big curly hair—specifically Farrah Fawcett hair, but I would settle for anything other than my mop of stringy noodles. Since professional salon prices were too steep for our family budget, the solution was obvious—the $6 home permanent. Every few months my mom would roll my molecularly fine hair around rollers, dump on some chemicals, and within an hour I would be left with a head that looked half Brillo pad, half dandelion-in-seed! Ohhhhh and the maintenance and the hair

products and hairpicks to keep this coif in its full glory. I do not have a single school picture as a teenager where I do not have this hair. I so wanted what others had and, in an effort to get it, I made some very bad choices. I didn't need a home perm—what I did need was a haircut that was suited to my active lifestyle and that made the most of my God-given hair.

I see this same thing happen with many new clients. No, they don't have home perms, but they have spent time, energy, and money trying to emulate a lifestyle that isn't theirs. They look inside their neighbor's house and yearn for similar spaces. They see a perfectly styled room in a magazine and they want to have one just like it. I point out to them that this magazine setting has been styled without a TV, without kids and their mountains of toys, without dogs/cats/guinea pigs or other drooling, scratching, shedding members of the family. The fact that the clients have one or all of the above means that we may have to rethink that white mohair sofa.

You can have a room that is beautiful and practical—it just starts with being really honest with yourself about your lifestyle. When I see a client for the first time, I tell them not to clean up—I want to see how they really live. That way I can see what the problems are and deal with the practical, functional side of things before I move onto the pretty stuff. Don't get me wrong, it's still OK—actually beneficial—to dream about the neighbor's beautiful kitchen or the designer living room that you saw in the

magazine. But rather than emulating it, ask yourself exactly what it is that you like about the room—is it the color, lighting, patterns, the furniture, the openness? All of these factors can be manipulated to some degree to suit your own personal tastes

LEFT THIS IS THE STRAIGHT, STRINGY HAIR I WAS BORN WITH. CENTER AND THIS IS THE HAIR I GAVE MYSELF (AGE 14). RIGHT MY DAUGHTER INHERITED BOTH MY HAIR AND MY LOVE OF LAUGHTER.

and lifestyle no matter what your budget. In the end you may not get that big head of curly hair, but you will get a style perfectly suited to you.

LIFE IS FUNNY—CONTRARY TO POPULAR BELIEF, THE BUSINESS OF INTERIOR DESIGN IS NOT GLAMOROUS. I don't know how many times I've told people what I do only to hear them say, "Interior design—oooooh, how glamorous!" That is usually followed by "my mother/father/ sister/uncle/parakeet is taking an interior design course." I bet my neighbors—one an account-

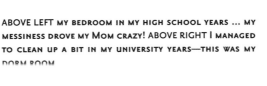

ABOVE LEFT MY BEDROOM IN MY HIGH SCHOOL YEARS ... MY MESSINESS DROVE MY MOM CRAZY! ABOVE RIGHT I MANAGED TO CLEAN UP A BIT IN MY UNIVERSITY YEARS—THIS WAS MY DORM ROOM

ant and the other a proctologist—never get this type of reaction when asked the same question. I truly believe that sometimes people think that all I do is show up at clients' houses, make a beeline for their gold cards, and swish around the world picking up exotic tchotchkes. I only wish it were that easy.

Don't get me wrong—I love what I do. When everything falls into place—a stimulating project that runs smoothly, with a healthy budget and great clients—it's magic. Those projects, however, especially when you are starting out, are few and far between. The true business of interior design is, well, just that— a business, and a tough, multifaceted one at that.

LIFE IS FUNNY—I HAVE SPENT YEARS BUILDING MY REPUTATION AS A SERIOUS, PROFESSIONAL DESIGNER ONLY TO FIND OUT I DON'T TAKE MYSELF TOO SERIOUSLY. I am, I admit, a bit wacky—not deranged, just wacky. There is nothing—absolutely nothing—that I enjoy more than having a good laugh, and everyone around me knows this. I've always thought it is important to show the serious side of design but not to take it too-o-o seriously—we're not talking brain surgery here! In a profession that stretches the saying "if anything can go wrong, it will" to its limits, sometimes all you can do is laugh to keep your sanity.

This is where I have to say that I have the best job in the world. I love seeing the reactions from clients when they see their new space for the first time, completely finished down to the last detail. I am lucky enough to work with a team of talented, hard-working people who manage to keep me—and each other— laughing. I am so blessed to be surrounded by a crew and team who are not only creative, but also just as wacky as I am. What a joy it is to do really great design work and have such a blast doing it. It may not be glamorous, but it certainly is fun!

LIFE IS FUNNY—ENJOY THE LAUGH!

KITCHENS

Welcome to my cook's tour! Feel free to borrow any of these design ingredients to whip up your own tasty kitchen redo.

A HAPPENING HUB

WHEN YOU WANT TO GATHER WITH FAMILY AND FRIENDS, THE KITCHEN CAN BECOME THE MAIN ATTRACTION WHEN IT HAS A WELCOMING LAYOUT AND DESIGN.

MAEVE AND PHILLIP'S HOUSE HAD PLENTY GOING for it with traditional features and charming personality. Unfortunately all that great character stopped short at the kitchen door. Floral wallpaper and an eye-crossing herringbone pattern on the floor made the room feel fussy, busy, and uninviting. An awkward layout compounded the unwelcoming feel. The couple's dream? To turn this space into a family-friendly hub where everyone—including their young son and a rambunctious dog—could relax and enjoy meals together.

The kitchen was a classic case of form following function, but the space desperately needed to work more efficiently. (The dishwasher wasn't even connected!) So I did some radical rethinking of the layout, carving out several well-contained areas that still would blend seamlessly together. I decided to flip the floor plan and switch the eating and kitchen areas, dividing them with a large peninsula.

BEFORE

Once the floor plan was outlined, we got started on the kitchen's fresh, new, contemporary look. For the main colors I chose creams and blues to brighten the room. Antique cream on the walls sets the stage for banks of creamy cabinets as well as new baseboards and crown molding. Handmade blue tiles lend

CREAM-HUED CABINETS ARE CLEAN, BRIGHT, AND SPACE-EXPANDING.
COLOR CHARACTER COMES FROM THE BACKSPLASH TILES.

OPPOSITE NIX USING A CABINET ABOVE THE RANGE HOOD AND EXPOSE THE SCULP-
TURAL BEAUTY OF THIS COMPONENT. RIGHT A TALL PANTRY CABINET IS CONVENIENT
TO THE WORK CORE AND THE BREAKFAST TABLE. BELOW I ENVISIONED A COZY BAN-
QUETTE WITH A LEDGE AND SHELVES FOR SHOWING OFF TREASURES.

color and pattern to the backsplash. A speckled denim-blue counter caps off the maple-finished island with more standout color. Vinyl flooring with a diagonal pattern of large cream and blue tiles takes color to the floor.

For the main fabric accents, I chose a striped pattern of blue, cream, green, and red, using it for throw pillows and a valance. We installed the valance slightly above the kitchen window to create the illusion of height.

Instead of floating the breakfast table in the center of the eating space, I designed a banquette framed by cupboards along one wall. Pulling the table up to the banquette leaves

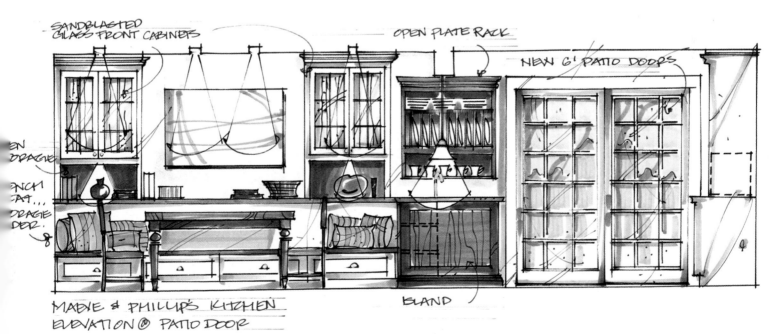

SANDBLASTED
GLASS FRONT CABINETS   OPEN PLATE RACK

NEW 6' PATIO DOORS

MABVE & PHILLIP'S KITCHEN
ELEVATION @ PATIO DOOR

ISLAND

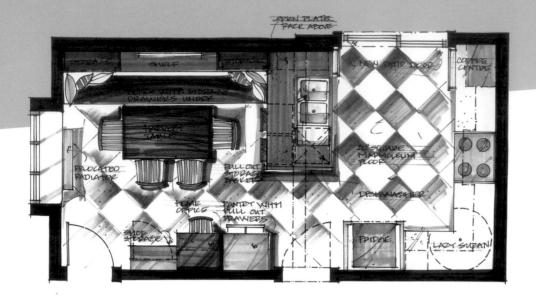

Labels on floor plan: OPEN PLATE RACK ABOVE; STORAGE; SHELF; STORAGE; BENCH WITH STORAGE DRAWERS UNDER; HARVEST TABLE; RELOCATED RADIATOR; SHOE STORAGE; HOME OFFICE; PANTRY WITH PULL OUT DRAWERS; PULL OUT STORAGE BASKETS; NEW PATIO DOOR; COFFEE CENTRE; 20" SQUARE MARMOLEUM FLOOR; DISHWASHER; FRIDGE; LAZY SUSAN

room on the opposite wall for a mini office with a desk and more storage space.

To remedy the kitchen's lack of lighting, we installed recessed lighting over work areas. Undercabinet fixtures focus task lighting on countertops and highlight the backsplash, while stainless-steel pendants illuminate the island. Over the table, a contemporary chandelier that matches the pendants brightens the area for meals.

Finishing touches include a modern, built-in coffeemaker, a blackboard-coated cupboard for grocery lists and memos, and several storage baskets and shelves. Now the kitchen is ready for Maeve and Phillip to welcome their family and friends for good times and great food.

KA-CHING, KA-CHING

THAT'S THE SOUND YOU'LL HEAR WHEN BUYING A BUILT-IN REFRIGERATOR. IT'S A WONDERFUL APPLIANCE, BUT IF ONE ISN'T IN YOUR BUDGET, DON'T WORRY. INSTEAD, PURCHASE A STANDARD, FREESTANDING REFRIGERATOR AND BUILD AN ENCLOSURE AROUND IT THAT MATCHES THE KITCHEN CABINETRY. YOU CAN TOP THE ENCLOSURE WITH CABINETS, AS SHOWN RIGHT, OR BUILD IN SHELVES FOR COOKBOOKS OR FOR DISPLAY. YOU ALSO COULD USE THE SPACE FOR A WINE RACK. YOUR APPROXIMATE SAVINGS? $7,200 FOR A BUILT-IN REFRIGERATOR VERSUS ABOUT $1,500 FOR THE FREESTANDING MODEL. PLENTY LEFT OVER FOR A NICE STACK OF PANCAKES!

ENTERTAINING IDEAS

A FLOWING LAYOUT, HANDSOME APPOINTMENTS, AND SPACE FOR FRIENDS
MAKE THIS BUNGALOW THE LIFE OF THE PARTY.

IT'S NOT THE SIZE OF THE SPACE THAT MAKES IT FIT for entertaining but how it's laid out. Jason's first home is a case in point: The small bungalow was downright cramped—not to mention "too cute" and outdated. Definitely not a hip hangout. I stepped in to create the illusion of space, design an efficient layout, and take the look from cute to cool.

To accomplish these goals, we knocked down walls separating the tiny kitchen from the boxy living room and dining room areas to make one large, loungelike space. I then chose matching fabrics and selected furniture and accents to ensure that the merged spaces worked together.

The colors for the new space were chosen for their chic yet decidedly masculine appeal—warm woods, neutral tones, and metallic accents. The draperies are subtly striped panels and sheers; the furniture and accent pillows pick up on the new metallic elements and soft shades. The look is sophisticated yet

BEFORE

neutral enough to grow with Jason as he adds personal touches to his new pad.

The '50s-style kitchen was small and lacked personality. So we tore out the bland white cabinets and countertops, eliminated the old appliances, and transformed the room with warm wood cabinetry, chic countertop surfaces, a faux stainless-steel backsplash, and modern stainless-steel appliances. Sleek graphic flooring replaced the old flooring.

A large island is the focal point, serving as a kind of traffic cop that divides the kitchen from the rest of the room. It also serves as a place where Jason's friends can sit and sip cocktails without getting underfoot while he cooks.

Above the island bar, an elegant wooden canopy adds architectural interest and serves as a base for recessed lighting and a trio of hip, hanging fixtures.

ABOVE Warm wood flooring defines the area for gathering and dining. LEFT An open design for the kitchen, living room, and dining area allows the space to flow as one large area for entertaining. OPPOSITE Metallic stools pull up to the island ledge so friends can converse with the cook and enjoy a drink.

SHINY METAL AND DARK WOOD TURN THIS BUNGALOW KITCHEN INTO A HIP,
SOPHISTICATED SPACE FOR ENTERTAINING.

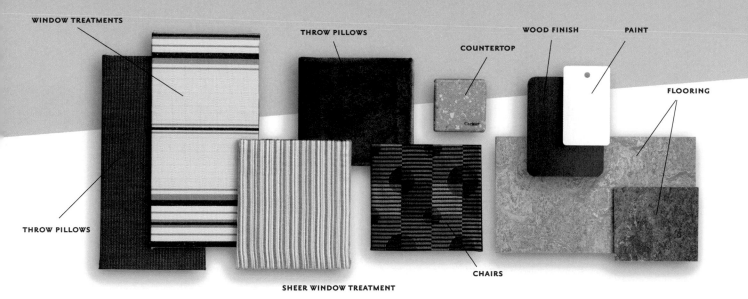

WINDOW TREATMENTS

THROW PILLOWS

COUNTERTOP

WOOD FINISH

PAINT

FLOORING

THROW PILLOWS

SHEER WINDOW TREATMENT

CHAIRS

Working with the main color scheme, I added some new furniture to the living and dining rooms. I also updated some of Jason's older pieces, including his white metal chairs that had ratty upholstery. These became ebony seats with striped cushions; a long, bland coffee table received a gleaming new surface of simulated stainless steel and glass.

To round out the redo, I introduced a variety of accents, including small stainless-steel kitchen appliances, an assortment of vases and bowls, a contemporary rug, and even a modish, artichokelike light fixture that brings a warm glow and sculptural beauty to the space.

The redesigned bungalow is still small, but it's definitely big on entertaining with ease and style.

UNLEVEL BEST

YOU WOULD BE AMAZED AT HOW UNLEVEL A CEILING IN AN OLDER HOME CAN BE. (WE'VE HAD CEILINGS THAT ARE OFF BY AS MUCH AS 3 INCHES IN A 10-FOOT SPAN!) SAVE YOUR INSTALLERS A NIGHTMARE, AND DON'T TAKE THE CABINETRY ALL THE WAY TO THE CEILING. INSTEAD, LEAVE AN INCH GAP BETWEEN THE TOP OF THE CABINETS AND THE CEILING. YOUR EYE ONLY READS THIS SPACE AS AN ATTRACTIVE SHADOW LINE, AND YOU GAIN SOME PLAY FOR THE IMPERFECTIONS OF THE CEILING.

OPPOSITE A LARGE ACCENT BOWL MIMICS THE SCALE OF THE PENDANT FIXTURE. TOP A COLLECTION OF DARK-NEUTRAL STRIPES, GEOMETRICS, AND SOLIDS MAKES A MASCULINE PALETTE FOR JASON'S BACHELOR PAD. ABOVE TWO TONES OF GRAY FLOORING IN A LARGE-SCALE GRAPHIC DESIGN REPEAT THE HUE OF METALLIC ACCENTS USED THROUGHOUT THE SPACES.

TRADITIONAL TUNE-UP

An off-key kitchen becomes a melodic, classic composition of creamy cabinetry and English country components.

IF YOUR LINOLEUM PREDATES DISCO, IT'S TIME TO do "the hustle" and shuffle it out of the house. In addition to 30-year-old flooring, Linda's kitchen suffered from poor lighting and banks of quintessentially 1970s flat-front, medium-brown cabinets. Linda longed for an updated yet traditional eat-in kitchen that would bring her family together at mealtimes. But to give this space a family-friendly facelift, we had to rip out and rebuild.

Except for the kitchen, Linda's home is Georgian in style, so an English country theme for the new kitchen was a natural choice. Before we made any cosmetic changes, however, I had to remedy some floor plan problems. The old kitchen was a big box with lots of wasted floor space. We replaced the windows to the right of the old stove with sliding doors that will lead to a future deck. To gain more useful counter space on each side of the stove, I created an angled

BEFORE

wall in what had been a dead corner and installed a new stove flanked by new cabinets and countertops.

Traditional raised-panel cabinetry in a timeless cream-color antique-glaze finish and pewter hardware establish an elegant tone. Durable porcelain tiles in shades of cream, putty, and tan

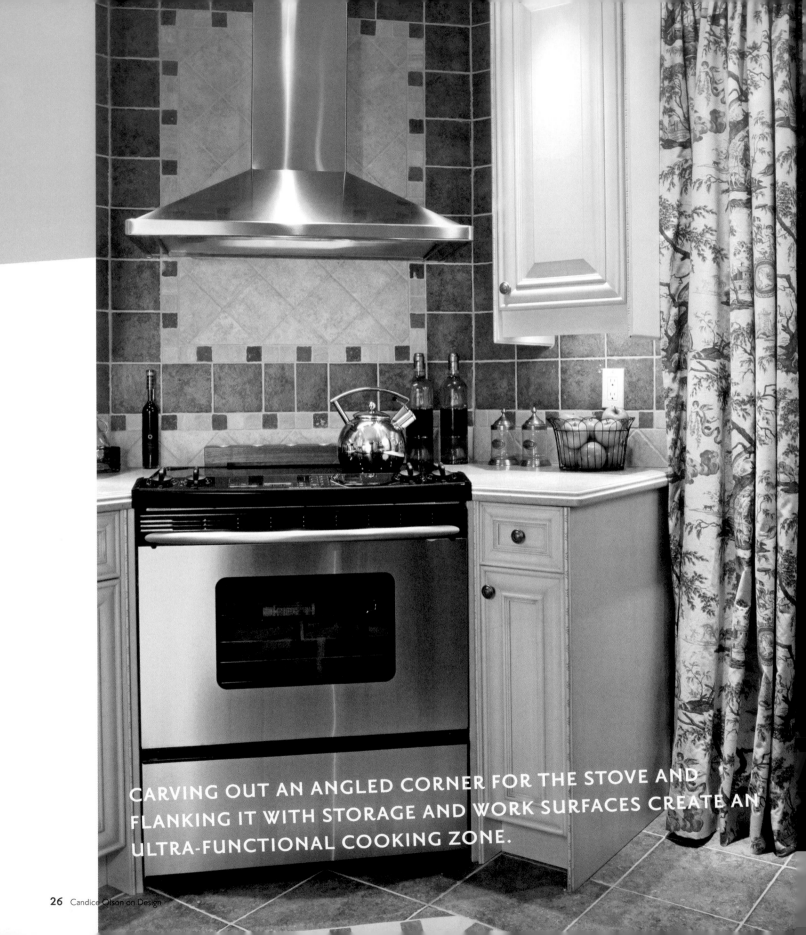

CARVING OUT AN ANGLED CORNER FOR THE STOVE AND FLANKING IT WITH STORAGE AND WORK SURFACES CREATE AN ULTRA-FUNCTIONAL COOKING ZONE.

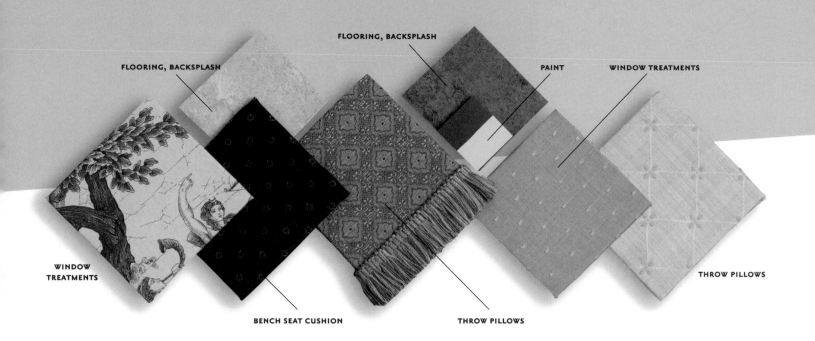

FLOORING, BACKSPLASH

FLOORING, BACKSPLASH

PAINT

WINDOW TREATMENTS

WINDOW TREATMENTS

THROW PILLOWS

BENCH SEAT CUSHION

THROW PILLOWS

grace the floor and backsplashes with understated style, visually linking these surfaces to the cabinetry. Solid-surfacing countertops frame the new, classic farm-style sink with its gooseneck faucet. Although wall space is limited in this kitchen, chocolate brown on the walls serves as a remarkable foil for the cabinetry, trim work, and tile.

To highlight these surfaces and components and give Linda plenty of task lighting, we replaced the old globe lights with new fixtures. Undercabinet lights illuminate work surfaces, and recessed fixtures wash light down from the ceiling. A wrought-iron chandelier over the dining table and sconces on the wall above the banquette give the eating area a

BANK ON BANQUETTES

I LOVE BANQUETTES—THEY PROVIDE OPTIMAL SEATING IN LESS SPACE BECAUSE THE LEGS FROM CHAIRS AND THE TABLE CAN BECOME TOO CROWDED. THE BENCH SEAT OFFERS A WONDERFUL OPPORTUNITY TO INTRODUCE COLOR WITH FABRIC-COVERED PILLOWS AND THE SEAT CUSHION. IF YOU HAVE KIDS, CHOOSE WASHABLE FABRICS AND PUT A ZIPPER IN THE CUSHION COVER SO YOU CAN TAKE IT OFF AND WASH IT WHEN NEEDED. KEEP IN MIND THAT PATTERNS CAN HIDE THOSE SPAGHETTI STAINS TOO! USE THE BENCH FOR ADDITIONAL STORAGE BY DESIGNING IT WITH A FLIP-UP SEAT OR PUTTING ACCESSIBLE STORAGE ALONG THE BENCH FRONT.

OPPOSITE STAINLESS-STEEL APPLIANCES, INCLUDING THE RANGE AND SCULPTURAL HOOD, INJECT A FEW MODERN NOTES INTO THIS CLASSICALLY INSPIRED KITCHEN. ABOVE AN OPEN PLATE RACK OVER THE DISHWASHER IS A VISUAL BREAK IN A WALL FULL OF CABINETRY.

cozy feeling and help define it as a separate zone within the kitchen space.

The fabrics in Linda's new kitchen pick up on the cream, putty, and tan in the tile. Elegant toile softens the sliding door and repeats in a valance on the window above the sink. This traditional fabric is the perfect accompaniment to the English country theme.

Because Linda wanted a traditional kitchen, the modern elements that I incorporated still blend with the overall look. Stainless-steel appliances relate to the gray tiles and blend into the background. An open plate rail above the dishwasher breaks up the wall of cabinets and shows off Linda's putty-color and amber dinnerware.

Linda's new space works hard, but it's also a comfortable gathering spot that brings everyone together at the table.

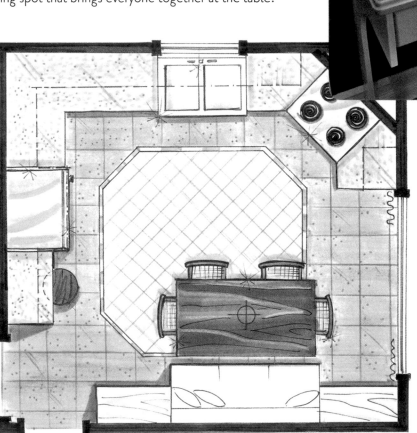

LEFT THIS AERIAL VIEW OF THE KITCHEN SHOWS THE NEWLY CONFIGURED CORNER FOR THE STOVE AND THE NEW BUILT-IN SEATING THAT ANCHORS THE EATING AREA. I USED CONTRASTING COLORS AND SIZES OF TILE TO CREATE THE "CARPET" EFFECT ON THE FLOOR. ABOVE A CONVENIENT MESSAGE CENTER REQUIRES ONLY A SLICE OF SPACE. OPPOSITE THE ELEGANT DINING TABLE AND SIMPLE WOODEN CHAIRS PAIR WITH A BUILT-IN BENCH THAT ALSO PROVIDES STORAGE.

TIME TRAVELER

YOU CAN TRANSPORT A KITCHEN INTO THE FUTURE TO ENJOY NOW AND ATTRACT PROSPECTIVE BUYERS LATER.

IT DEFINITELY WAS TIME FOR BRIDGET AND DOUG to head back to the future. They had just finished a 12-year stint in a time warp of sorts, making do with a stark white 1970s kitchen with failing cabinetry and an unattractive fluorescent lighted ceiling. While they were ready to update the kitchen, they also expected to be selling the house in a few years (their children were almost grown). With that in mind, the new kitchen would need to attract prospective buyers.

There was nothing worth keeping in this space, so we gutted the room and started anew. Since the kitchen adjoins the family room, I chose a color scheme that allows the two spaces to flow seamlessly—a palette of leather-tan, ebony, silvery gray-blue, and stainless steel.

Color begins at the floor with tile laid in a checkerboard pattern. Installing the tile on the diagonal creates the impression that this galley-style space is wider than it is.

BEFORE

Cabinetry does more than anything else to define a room's style. I chose traditional cherry cabinets because the look is timeless and likely to appeal to future buyers. To introduce a more contemporary edge to the kitchen, we accented some of the upper cabinets with smoky glass door inserts. Black solid-surfacing countertops repeat

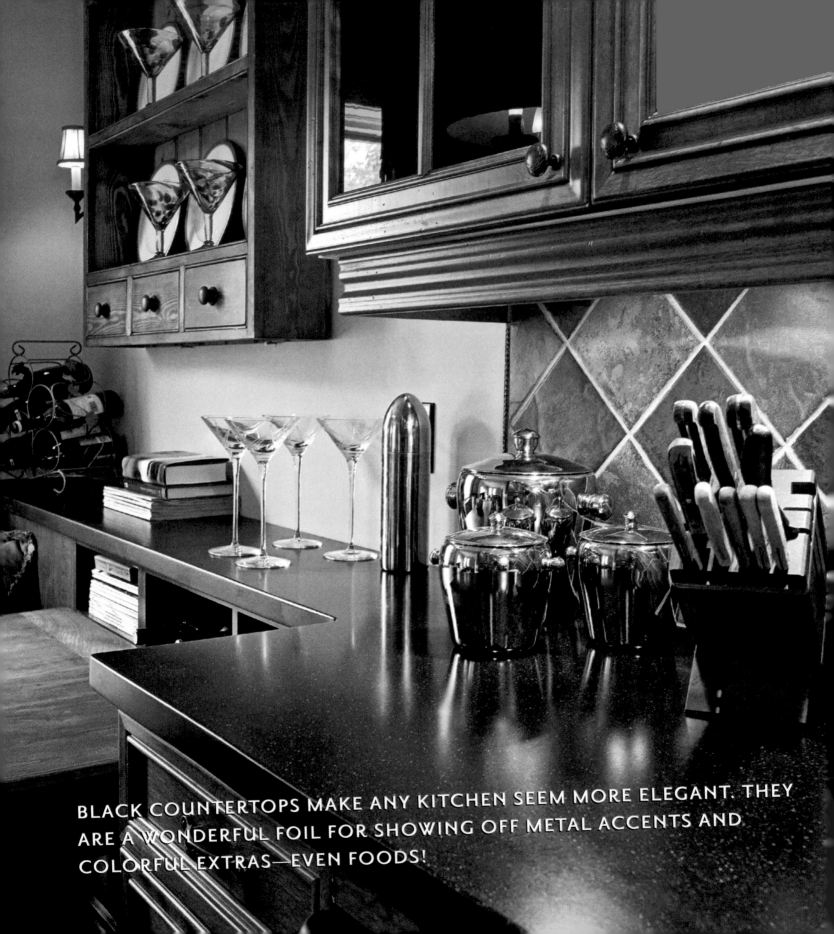

BLACK COUNTERTOPS MAKE ANY KITCHEN SEEM MORE ELEGANT. THEY ARE A WONDERFUL FOIL FOR SHOWING OFF METAL ACCENTS AND COLORFUL EXTRAS—EVEN FOODS!

OPPOSITE Continuing a narrow slice of countertop along the wall creates a niche for the dining table and provides space for display. RIGHT Recessed halogen fixtures along the perimeter of the room and undercabinet lights ensure plenty of illumination for cooking.

the dark beauty of the glass; backsplash tiles tie in with the look of the floor. Stainless-steel appliances and a new sink with a built-in drainboard contribute a sparkling touch to a kitchen that was positively starving for attention!

The old fluorescent ceiling was replaced with several types of lighting fixtures. In the kitchen work core, recessed halogens punctuate the ceiling perimeter, shining down on counters and cabinetry. Undercabinet lighting is functional and highlights the texture of the backsplash tile. In the eating area, sconces and a chandelier cast a soft, warm glow over casual meals with family and friends.

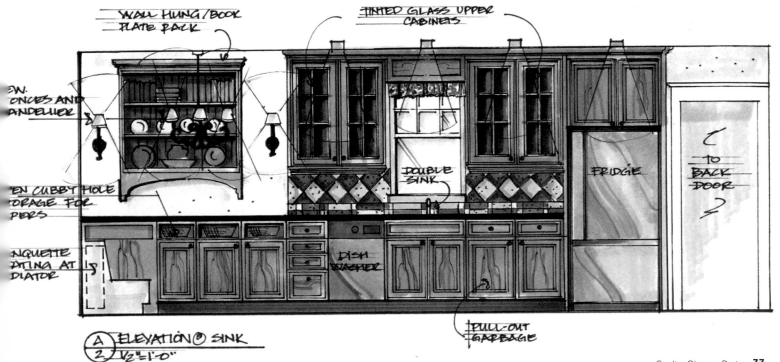

WALL HUNG / BOOK PLATE RACK

TINTED GLASS UPPER CABINETS

NEW SCONCES AND CHANDELIER

OPEN CUBBY HOLE STORAGE FOR PAPERS

BANQUETTE SEATING AT RADIATOR

DOUBLE SINK

DISH WASHER

FRIDGE

TO BACK DOOR

PULL-OUT GARBAGE

A ELEVATION @ SINK
2   1/2"=1'-0"

FLOOR TILE   BACKSPLASH TILE   BACKSPLASH TILE   FLOOR TILE

PAINT   BACKSPLASH DETAIL TILE   THROW PILLOWS   BENCH SEAT CUSHION

ABOVE INSTALLING THE FLOOR TILES ON THE DIAGONAL MAKES THE ROOM APPEAR WIDER. RECESSED LIGHTS IN THE CEILING FOLLOW THE PERIMETER OF THE ROOM, WASHING LIGHT ON THE CABINET DOORS AND COUNTERTOP WORK AREAS. OPPOSITE THE BUILT-IN BENCH PUTS AN OLD RADIATOR UNDER WRAPS AND TURNS THIS END OF THE ROOM INTO A COZY CORNER FOR DINING.

In the dining nook, a built-in bench seat disguises the old radiator (no longer functioning) and supplies space-saving seating. A new wooden table, a couple of country-French-style chairs, and a wall-hung antique pine hutch anchor this end of the long kitchen. Because the style of the room is traditional but not formal or fussy, I kept the window treatments simple: straight panels with a pinch-pleat header at the dining end of the room and a matching valance at the window over the sink.

Today, the old white kitchen is a foggy memory, replaced by a space with timeless appeal.

CABINET CHARACTER

AN ABUNDANCE OF SOLID CABINET DOORS CAN OVERPOWER A KITCHEN. TO CREATE VISUAL RELIEF AND ARCHITECTURAL INTEREST, MIX IT UP WITH A FEW STYLISH DEPARTURES. ONE STRATEGY IS TO VARY THE HEIGHTS AND DEPTHS OF THE CABINETS. YOU ALSO CAN CHANGE OUT SOLID-FACE CABINETS WITH RACKS THAT STORE DISHES OR WINE AND OPEN SHELVES FOR DISPLAYING COLLECTIONS OR STORING COOKBOOKS. OR TRANSFORM UPPER DOORS BY ADDING GLASS INSERTS. IF YOU PREFER THAT PEOPLE DON'T SEE YOUR PEANUT BUTTER, USE GLASS THAT IS SANDBLASTED OR REEDED SO THAT THE CONTENTS OF THE CABINETS ARE OBSCURED.

DESIGN ESSENTIALS: KITCHENS

THESE ARE MY FAVORITE INGREDIENTS FOR A KITCHEN THAT'S REALLY COOKIN' WITH GOOD LOOKS AND SMART FUNCTION.

① COSMETIC VS. COMPLETE

Kitchen redos typically fall into two categories: a work core that you can refresh cosmetically or a kitchen that needs a complete overhaul.

The typical cosmetic candidate might be a '50s or '60s-style kitchen with a layout that works really well and with cabinets in good condition. In these cases, look at ways to update the finishes and surfaces to erase the outdated look.

The kitchen requiring a complete overhaul is beyond hope—maybe it's falling apart with no redeeming qualities. The ship is sinking, but rather than jump ship, you can do a to-the-studs remodeling.

BEFORE

In real life, large and small redos are budget driven. The good news is that your choices are tremendous. (You could spend $200 or $2,000 on a sink!) Shop wisely and decide which features are most important,

and rank them by priority. You'll find what you want at a price you can afford. You can manipulate the budget by replacing expensive materials with a lower cost look-alike (granite versus look-alike laminate, for example). By giving up one luxury feature (say, a wine refrigerator), you can invest the money in another component that may fall higher on your list (such as a second sink).

ABOVE AND RIGHT THE STRUCTURE OF DIANE'S KITCHEN WAS SOLID, BUT THE SURFACES NEEDED UPDATING. PAINTING THE BLOND OAK CABINETS WITH A WALNUT FINISH—UP TO THE CEILING—CREATES THE ILLUSION OF NEW CUSTOM CABINETS. FLOORING, COUNTERTOPS, BACKSPLASHES, AND APPLIANCES ARE ALL NEW TO ENSURE A THOROUGH COSMETIC REDO.

LEFT A CENTRAL LIGHTING FIXTURE ONCE CAST HARSH FLUORESCENT LIGHT THAT WASN'T FLATTERING TO PEOPLE OR FOOD. I TOOK IT DOWN AND STRATEGICALLY INSTALLED HALOGEN RECESSED FIXTURES TO ILLUMINATE CABINET FRONTS AND INTERIORS AS WELL AS WORK AREAS.

homely central light fixture with a track-lighting system. Outfit the track with five or six halogen heads so you can beam light around the kitchen—rather than suffer with one bulb in the middle of the ceiling that doesn't accent or shine anywhere.

It's also important to install undercabinet lighting so that you have additional illumination for your perimeter countertops. The front face of the cabinets should hide the fixtures, which should be positioned close to the front of the cabinets. For undercabinet fixtures, you can use either low-voltage halogens or fluorescent tubes. If you use halogens, put them on a separate dimmer switch so that you can leave them on at night for a gentle glow. Small lights tucked into the toekicks of your cabinets (that's the niche near the floor) make wonderful, serene nightlights.

② LIGHTING: THE GOOD, THE BAD, AND THE VERY UGLY

Good or bad lighting makes or breaks a kitchen. Properly positioned, lighting can make wood tones glow, sculpt cabinet details, lend drama to painted finishes, and make that stainless steel hood sparkle. Position recessed fixtures relatively close to the cabinet fronts—about 12 inches from the faces and centered on the cabinet doors—so they illuminate countertop work areas as well as cabinet interiors. (Be forewarned that contractors often worry that the lights are too close to cabinetry, but they're not. Trust me.)

If you're only doing a cosmetic redo, consider replacing a

BEFORE

③ THE CASE FOR CABINETS

Cabinets may be one of the more costly components for your kitchen (unless you spend a fortune on appliances!). Here are some considerations to help you get a look you'll love:

WHITE OR WOOD? You already may know whether you want stained or painted cabinets or your budget may decide for you: White painted cabinets are definitely less expensive than exotic woods such as Brazilian cherry.

SNIP AND CLIP. If you're having trouble deciding between stained or painted cabinets, flip through decorating and kitchen magazines and tear out examples of spaces you like. You'll note recurring themes that will help you know which style and finish to choose.

MIX IT UP. Introduce variety by including a mix of solid cabinet doors, glass-panel doors, and open shelves. If you don't want people to see your olive

oil, select textured or translucent glass panels or back the glass with fabric.

In an "unfitted" kitchen, the cabinetry appears to have evolved over time as you gathered a piece here and a piece there. An easy way to achieve this look is to introduce a kitchen island in a different style and finish from the perimeter cabinetry—bringing an island with beautiful carved legs into a contemporary kitchen, for example. This immediately softens the hard lines of a modern space.

As an alternative, paint perimeter cabinetry one color and the island another. Or paint the cabinetry and stain the island. For still more diversity, consider painting upper cabinets one color and lower cabinets a complementary shade.

You also can hang upper cabinets at varying heights to create interest. Or pull some pieces of lower cabinetry forward to add dimension. Brackets and turned pieces added beneath upper cabinets and "legs" tucked into the toe kicks of lower cabinets create the look of furniture.

LEFT THE OLD CABINETS WERE PRIMED, PAINTED, AND GIVEN A STRIATED FINISH TO LOOK LIKE FADED BLUE JEANS. A STAINLESS-STEEL-AND-WOOD CENTER ISLAND LENDS VARIETY. ABOVE OPEN SHELVES PREVENT THIS BANK OF CABINETRY FROM OVERPOWERING THE ROOM.

- If you don't care for laminate, you still can have stone on a budget, but use 12×12 tiles instead of a slab and trim the countertop with wood for a finished edge. For easy cleaning, keep grout joints to a minimum. If you love the look of a slab, use it on your island and opt for granite tiles for perimeter countertops.

- Some choices, such as limestone and marble, are beautiful but porous and can be stained by liquids such as wine or tomato juice. Sealers are available to inhibit stains, and darker versions of porous stone hide some spills.

- Although many people warned me away from wood countertops, I have one and I love it. If you can be a bit forgiving, this surface can warm up a kitchen.

- Stainless-steel countertops are virtually indestructible and super hygienic, but your kitchen will look like a spaceship if you use too many. In this case, as with most countertop materials, you can create a better look if you use a mix of materials. The island is a good place to use a countertop that's different from perimeter ones.

LEFT HERE'S AN UNEXPECTED USE OF A COMMON MATERIAL: THE LONG COUNTERTOP IN THE FOREGROUND IS RECOVERED IN DURABLE, HARD WEARING LINOLEUM SHEET FLOORING IN A FUN SHADE OF ORANGE. IT PAYS TO THINK OUTSIDE THE PACKAGING. BELOW BLACK COUNTERTOPS REPLACE WHITE ONES IN THIS KITCHEN TO INCREASE THE DRAMA. THE DARK SURFACE ALSO DOES A FANTASTIC JOB OF SHOWING OFF FOOD AND DISHWARE.

④ COUNTERTOP CLASS

You'll find a vast variety of countertop materials from which to choose. Here are some things I've learned about countertop surfaces over the years:

- If granite is in your budget, it's a beautiful, hard wearing choice that even accepts hot pots and won't scratch if your knife slips. Synthetic quartz is also incredibly hard and durable. Granite and quartz can be worth the investment if you do a lot of cooking and chopping.

- If you have a tight budget, there are lots of fabulous laminates that give you the look of granite, marble, limestone, quartz, or other materials. Keep in mind that laminate is not as hard wearing as solid surfacing or stone.

BEFORE

DINE, GATHER

WHETHER YOUR DECORATING STYLE IS ELEGANT OR CASUAL, YOU CAN DESIGN YOUR LIVING ROOM, DINING ROOM, AND FAMILY ROOM TO SAY "WELCOME! RELAX! ENJOY!"

RELAX

BACKPACKS TO BEAUTY

IF YOUR FORMAL DINING ROOM IS ATTRACTING ONLY KIDS AND BACKPACKS, MAKE IT ENTICING FOR ELEGANT DINNERS WITH A DRAMATIC REDO LIKE THIS ONE.

RUTH'S DINING ROOM HAD ALL THE ELEMENTS OF an exquisite formal space worthy of elegant black-tie dinners: deep egg-and-dart crown molding, high paneled wainscoting, full-length leaded-glass windows, and classical corner niches. Unfortunately, the pale putty-and-gold color scheme and skimpy red-patterned draperies were so boring that all Ruth could see was "three shades of blah." The room left her cold, so she left it alone—and before long, the kids took over the room, dumping books and homework there, along with skateboards, sports equipment, and other gear.

To help Ruth take back the dining room and create a beautiful space for hosting intimate dinners, we banished the kids and tackled the blahs.

Color was key to this transformation. Rich chocolate brown covers both walls and paneling, and a dark bronze glaze over the paint adds metallic highlights. The subtle shimmer gives

BEFORE

the walls the look of dark walnut paneling and positively glows under candlelight! The niches, crown molding, and ceiling are painted ivory for a crisp contrast that keeps all the brown from feeling too weighty. Next came lighting: New recessed fixtures spotlight key areas in the room, including the decorative niches.

I LIKE TO FINISH DINING CHAIRS WITH MORE THAN ONE FABRIC. THIS CREATES INTEREST AND MAKES THE CHAIRS LOOK BEAUTIFUL FROM EVERY VANTAGE POINT.

A grand, swirly chandelier replaces the old skimpy lighting fixture and hangs lower to better fill the area above the table.

Since this room will be at its best at night, I wanted to make the most of the sparkle factor. To reflect light and enhance the illusion of depth and space, I covered the wall between the niches with mirror. To pick up on the gridlike effect of the panels in the wainscoting, I created a pattern with different-size pieces of mirror and marked the intersections with decorative rosettes.

The style of Ruth's dining table and chairs suited the new look of the dining room, but the old upholstery had to go. Instead of recovering the chairs in a single fabric, I chose three for each chair—an enlarged Asian style medallion on the back

WALL CLAD IN MIRROR PANELS

SPOTLIGHT NICHE

A ELEVATION
2 1/2"=1'0"

NEW 67" LONG BUFFET

OPPOSITE ARTWORK IN MUSEUM-STYLE GILT FRAMES REINFORCES THE OLD-WORLD LOOK OF THE ROOM. TALL VASES IN THE NICHES CAN HOLD FRESH FLOWERS, FRUITS, OR SEASONAL DECORATIONS. LEFT A MIRRORED PANEL ACCENTS THE TRADITIONAL ARCHITECTURE. ABOVE GATHERING TWO FABRICS ONTO ONE ROD GIVES THE APPEARANCE OF DOUBLE-LAYERED DRAPERIES.

PAINT

ANTIQUE PERSIAN RUG

CHAIR SEAT UPHOLSTERY FABRIC

OUTSIDE CHAIR BACK
UPHOLSTERY FABRIC

WINDOW
TREATMENT

PAINT TREATMENT SAMPLE

DRAPERY DETAIL

INSIDE CHAIR BACK UPHOLSTERY FABRIC

WINDOW TREATMENT

rests, a small print on the back side, and a solid velvet on the seats. When you look at them from different angles, the fabrics work together to pull in all the colors from the room.

To complete the atmosphere of old-world elegance, I found a new buffet for the mirrored wall and a Chinese cabinet that serves as a bar. Two cinnamon-color chairs flank the cabinet. An antique Persian rug brings the color on the walls to the floor and wraps the room in glorious style.

Rescued from backpacks and skateboards, Ruth's dining room is a warm cocoon of elegance—the perfect setting for memorable gatherings.

HALOGEN FOR SPARKLE

I ENCOURAGE THE USE OF HALOGEN FIXTURES RATHER THAN INCANDESCENT LIGHT—ESPECIALLY IN THE DINING ROOM. THIS LIGHT SOURCE WAS ORIGINALLY PRIZED BY JEWELRY STORES BECAUSE HALOGEN PULLS OUT THE NATURAL SPARKLE OF DIAMONDS. NOW IMAGINE THE SAME PRINCIPLE AT WORK IN YOUR DINING ROOM. YOUR FINE CRYSTAL, CHINA, AND SILVERWARE WILL LOOK FABULOUS! TO ENHANCE THE LIGHTING EFFECTS IN RUTH'S DINING ROOM, I ADDED MIRRORS TO ONE END WALL. INSTANTLY, THE ROOM GOT A BIG BURST OF BRIGHTNESS AS THE MIRRORS THREW BACK THE LIGHT FROM THE CHANDELIER AND THE RECESSED FIXTURES.

ABOVE MIRROR PANELS BEHIND THE BUFFET CREATE AN ILLUSION OF GREATER SPACE IN THE ROOM; DECORATIVE ROSETTES LEND MORE INTEREST WHERE THE PANELS INTERSECT. THE PORTRAIT SEEMS TO FLOAT AGAINST THE MIRRORED WALL. OPPOSITE THIS BEAUTIFUL CHINESE CABINET DOUBLES AS A BAR. THE CABINET'S DECORATIVE PAINT WORK AND THE COLOR OF THE FLANKING CHAIRS REALLY POP AGAINST THE DARK WALL.

Candice Olson on Design **47**

DIVINE DINING

ONCE A HOST TO CLUTTER, THIS ELEGANT AND ROMANTIC DINING ROOM
IS READY FOR BIG FAMILY-STYLE BANQUETS.

AS A HANDY-DANDY DUMPING GROUND FOR sewing machines, storage boxes, and all manner of odds and ends, the dining room in Andrea and Greg's multilevel home was rarely used. They wanted to play host to their large, extended family for eating extravaganzas, but before that could happen, they needed help: a dining room that could suit a family of four and a multigenerational gathering of 20.

The space was full of outdated features, from the old stucco ceiling to the pink '80s-style carpet. Aside from three pieces the couple wanted to keep—a dining room table, an antique hutch, and an embroidery made by Andrea's grandmother—this room would need a total top-to-bottom makeover.

Although we were stuck with the awkwardly angled ceiling, I turned it into a positive feature with character by covering it with beaded-board paneling and batten-board trim. Angled

BEFORE

recessed lighting fixtures pierce the new ceiling surface, washing atmospheric light onto the walls.

The dull lemon yellow on the walls gave way to a relaxing robin's egg blue. The ghastly pink carpet went to the dump and was replaced with a combination of hardwood flooring and

sculptured carpet. The dark-stained, oak hardwood floor forms a border for the embossed leaf rug inset into the middle. The fireplace needed a facelift too—it went from icky pink to bright white, and I added a purchased shelf to serve as a mantel. With a mirror above and candlesticks on the mantel, the fireplace anchors one end of the room as an appealing focal point.

Fabrics give the space a generous dose of traditional elegance. At the windows, side panels of a blue and brown floral pattern are accented with brown linen bands and beaded trim. Layered under these panels are simple linen sheers that filter light and a seagrass-and-silk blind that lends textural interest.

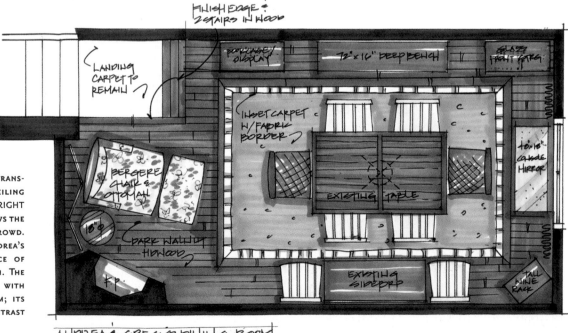

ABOVE BEADED-BOARD PANELING TRANS-FORMED THE ANGLED, STUCCO CEILING INTO AN ARCHITECTURAL FEATURE. RIGHT THE AERIAL VIEW OF THE ROOM SHOWS THE PLAN FOR ACCOMMODATING A CROWD. OPPOSITE THE EMBROIDERY BY ANDREA'S GRANDMOTHER OCCUPIES A PLACE OF HONOR AT ONE END OF THE ROOM. THE DARK WOOD SCREEN HARMONIZES WITH THE OTHER WOODS IN THE ROOM; ITS CLEAN, CONTEMPORARY LINES CONTRAST NICELY WITH THE CURVY CHAIR.

IF YOU HAVE A SPACIOUS DINING ROOM, INCLUDE A CHAISE OR A CHAIR AND OTTOMAN SO THE ROOM CAN BE USED FOR READING AND RELAXING AS WELL AS FOR DINING.

ROMAN BLINDS

TASSEL TRIM DETAIL

AREA RUG

CHAIR SEAT UPHOLSTERY FABRIC

END CHAIR UPHOLSTERY FABRIC

PAINT

DRAPERY SHEERS

FLOORING

CHAIR BACK UPHOLSTERY AND DRAPERY FABRIC

OPPOSITE A CONSOLE IN FRONT OF THE WINDOWS ANCHORS THIS END OF THE ROOM AND PROVIDES STORAGE AND DISPLAY SPACE. ABOVE ON THE ANTIQUE HUTCH, CLEAR DECORATIVE JARS HOLD SEA URCHINS AND SEASHELLS FOR A SUMMERTIME ACCESSORY. IN OTHER SEASONS, ANDREA AND GREG CAN FILL THESE JARS WITH PINECONES, GREENERY, OR FRUITS FOR INTERESTING AND EYE-PLEASING ACCENTS.

Upholstery on the new dining chairs reinforces the blue and brown color scheme with a mix of three fabrics—the floral and a stripe on the side chairs and a two-tone geometric on the end chairs. An armchair in the same beautiful floral sits beside the fireplace, where I placed a folding screen to form a nook for reading or napping after dinner.

Candlesticks, baskets, books, and pictures add the finishing touches that make the room more interesting for even the most demanding dinner guests. Now Andrea and Greg can welcome the multitudes or just a few cousins to a space that's clearly—and comfortably—a room for dining.

TABLE TALK

MY PREFERRED SHAPE FOR A DINING ROOM TABLE IS ROUND BECAUSE AT A RECTANGULAR TABLE YOU ONLY CAN VISIT WITH THE PEOPLE NEXT TO YOU. AT A ROUND TABLE, YOU CAN CONVERSE WITH EVERYONE; YOU ALSO CAN SEAT MORE PEOPLE "IN THE ROUND." IF YOUR ROOM LAYOUT DEMANDS A RECTANGULAR TABLE, CONSIDER ONE SUPPORTED BY A CENTER PEDESTAL OR TRESTLE. THE LACK OF LEGS AT THE CORNERS INCREASES YOUR SEATING OPTIONS, ALLOWING YOU TO POSITION CHAIRS ALL AROUND.

BELOW Sparse furnishings made this large combination living room and dining room unwelcoming. OPPOSITE Together with the dark wood floor, the metallic blue walls make the large room seem warm and cozy.

INTIMATE GATHERINGS

WRAPPING A LARGE COMBINATION GATHERING SPACE—IN THIS CASE, A LIVING ROOM/DINING ROOM—IN RICH COLOR MAKES AN INVITING BEGINNING.

THIS ROOM SHOULD HAVE BEEN PARTY CENTRAL— with generous space for conversation and dining, it easily could accommodate a large crowd. But the sparse furnishings and bland color scheme made it feel cavernous and stark. Even Mark and Julia didn't want to hang out in here, much less invite guests to join them. Their goal was to make this space live up to its potential, to be both grand and intimate—and personal.

To establish intimacy, I started with the shell of the room: Out went the broadloom carpeting, and in its place we installed dark, prefinished hardwood flooring. To shrink the room visually, I chose a metallic-blue striated finish for the walls. Dark floors and dark walls accented by crisp white woodwork successfully evoke a formal look that also feels warm and inviting.

The new color scheme, built around these elements, introduces a rich mix of chocolate brown, gunmetal blue, bronze,

BEFORE

and teal. New fabrics play up the scheme. At the windows, for example, luxurious bronze panels overlay floor-length sheers. Blue upholstery fabric and a deep bronze glaze on the wood frames refresh a pair of Mark and Julia's French chairs. These fabrics repeat on throw pillows in the living room.

IN ROOMS DEVOTED TO SPECIAL OCCASIONS, THE WINDOW TREATMENTS SHOULD REFLECT THE CELEBRATORY NATURE OF THE GATHERING.

To break up the long fireplace wall, I hung four mirrored panels, two framing the fireplace and two flanking the dining room china cabinet. Bordered in chocolate wood, each has a sconce fitted through the mirror. The result is an abundance of light reflected through the room. Along with this reflected light, updated fixtures create just the right atmosphere for conversation. Recessed lighting around the edges of the room provides overall illumination. Since this is such a large space, I added floor outlets so Mark and Julia could have table lamps in the center of the room as well as along the walls. Table lamps and floor lamps create cozy

A / 3 MARK & JULIA'S LIVING/DINING ROOM 1/2"=1'-0"

PORTABLE CAST STONE FIREPLACE

6'0" TOTAL SCONCE

DRAPERY FABRIC

PAINT

DRAPERY FABRIC

PAINT TREATMENT SAMPLE

DINING END CHAIR
UPHOLSTERY FABRIC

DRAPERY SHEERS

DINING HUTCH

THROW PILLOWS

THROW PILLOWS

THROW PILLOWS

pools of light, and a grand chandelier sparkles over the dining table. For a little visual surprise, I hung an understated pendant fixture over the coffee table. It calls attention to the conversation area—and might even serve as a conversation starter!

To encourage conversation in the living room and lingering at the dining table, I chose a collection of comfortable upholstered chairs in classic and contemporary styles. An Art Deco-inspired china cabinet and modern tables and sculptures complete the mix. The result? An intimate retreat that sets the stage for drama and elegant entertaining.

FIREPLACE ANYWHERE

MARK AND JULIA WERE TIRED OF THE FAUX FIREPLACE THEY HAD INHERITED FROM THE PREVIOUS OWNERS. SO WE DECIDED TO THROW OUT THE FAUX AND REPLACE IT WITH A PORTABLE FIREPLACE MADE FROM CAST STONE (SEE PAGE 56). THIS UNIT DOES NOT REQUIRE VENTING, AND DINNER PARTY GUESTS WILL LOVE RELAXING BESIDE ITS REAL FLAMES. THE FIREPLACE BURNS CANISTERS OF GEL MADE FROM SUGARCANE AND CORN. THIS GEL BURNS CLEANLY AND EMITS JUST A BIT OF WATER VAPOR. THE CAST STONE SURROUND ADDS ELEGANCE TO THIS ROOM, AND THE GEL CANISTERS MAKE HAVING A FIREPLACE A POSSIBILITY FOR EVERYONE.

ABOVE THIS THROW PULLS THE COLOR PALETTE OF CHOCOLATE BROWN, GUNMETAL BLUE, AND BRONZE TO THE SEATING AREA. OPPOSITE THE HANDSOME DINING TABLE AND CHAIRS COMFORTABLY ACCOMMODATE A SIT-DOWN DINNER FOR EIGHT.

A MARRIAGE OF TASTES

YOU LONG FOR ONE STYLE AND YOUR SPOUSE WANTS ANOTHER. HERE'S A
REDO THAT STRIKES A PEACEFUL BALANCE BETWEEN THE TWO.

WHAT DO YOU DO WHEN YOU LOVE ONE STYLE and your spouse leans toward another? That was the case when we stepped into the picture to redesign Andrew and Lisa's 1980s living room. While Lisa prefers warm French country decor, Andrew loves all things modern! I set out to meld the styles into one cohesive look.

Key to creating this dual-style redo is a faux stone veneer that we installed along one wall. The rough, irregular stone strikes the perfect balance, suggesting both an industrial loft and a cozy French cottage—which plays to the tastes of both Andrew and Lisa.

For the remaining surfaces, I used the stone veneer as inspiration. Fresh white paint brightens the wood ceiling, and pale ocher gives the walls a restful feel. Shades of putty and cream used elsewhere throughout the space complement the ocher hue.

BEFORE

Custom cabinetry creates lots of room for display, storage, and even additional seating. Two tall, putty-color storage units frame a built-in bench that is covered in custom upholstery fabric. This piece looks like a sofa and functions as one, providing extra seating when friends come over. The skirt hides storage shelves.

IN AN OPEN SPACE DESIGNED FOR MULTIPLE ACTIVITIES, USE FURNITURE GROUPINGS, VARIATIONS IN FLOORING, LIGHT FIXTURES, AND AREA RUGS TO DEFINE AREAS FOR SEATING, DINING, AND OTHER FUNCTIONS.

OPPOSITE **New**, PREFINISHED HARDWOOD FLOORING VISUALLY WARMS THE ROOM. RIGHT **Various** SHADES OF LATEX GLAZE HIGHLIGHT SOME OF THE "STONES" ON THE WALL, EMPHASIZING THE COLOR AND TEXTURE.

Andrew's flat-screen TV is mounted in the wall above the bench. Because it takes up no floor space or even shelf space, a flat-screen TV is the perfect solution for a long, narrow room like this one.

To bring this space to life, I chose recessed lights for general lighting. They pierce the narrow bulkhead that runs above the built-in cabinets and wash the stone wall from a hidden trough. New, updated track lights let Andrew and Lisa spotlight artwork or various areas of the room. Over the dining table, electric candlelight twinkles from a wrought iron chandelier. The fixtures are on dimmer switches so Lisa and Andrew

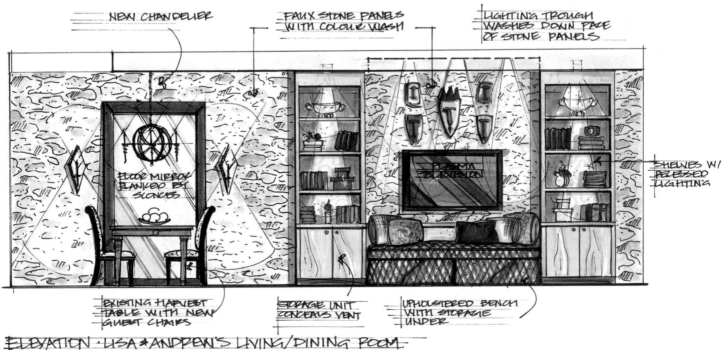

NEW CHANDELIER

FAUX STONE PANELS WITH COLOUR WASH

LIGHTING TROUGH WASHES DOWN FACE OF STONE PANELS

FLOOR MIRROR FLANKED BY SCONCES

PLASMA TELEVISION

SHELVES W/ RECESSED LIGHTING

EXISTING HARVEST TABLE WITH NEW GUEST CHAIRS

STORAGE UNIT CONCEALS VENT

UPHOLSTERED BENCH WITH STORAGE UNDER

ELEVATION · LISA & ANDREW'S LIVING/DINING ROOM

ENTRY FLOOR TILE

BENCH AND OCCASIONAL CHAIR UPHOLSTERY

FLOORING

DINING CHAIR UPHOLSTERY FABRIC

THROW PILLOWS

WINDOW TREATMENT TRIM

WINDOW TREATMENT

SOFA

PAINT

can create any ambience they like, depending on whether the occasion is formal or casual.

Fabric also helps blend the two decorating styles. Vintage-inspired fabrics that speak to Lisa's tastes actually work quite well with modern geometric prints, solids, and stripes that appeal to Andrew.

We also compromised between Andrew's and Lisa's decorating styles by bringing in a balance of furniture. The modern, clean lines of some pieces meet the traditional, comfortable lines of others. The result is a harmonious merging of time-worn traditional decor and clean, contemporary style.

CABINET CLASS

IN A ROOM WHERE MORE THAN ONE ACTIVITY TAKES PLACE, DESIGN CABINETRY TO PERFORM A NUMBER OF FUNCTIONS. CLOSED CABINETS CAN HOUSE MEDIA COMPONENTS (STEREO, TELEVISION, DVD PLAYER) AS WELL AS BOARD AND COMPUTER GAMES, DVDS, VIDEOS, AND CDS. OPEN SHELVES ARE HANDY FOR DISPLAYING COLLECTIONS AND PHOTOGRAPHS AND FOR ORGANIZING BOOKS. WHEN THE TELEVISION IS TOO BIG TO HIDE INSIDE A CABINET (AND WHO WANTS TO CONCEAL A COSTLY AND BEAUTIFUL FLAT-SCREEN MODEL?), CONSIDER FLANKING THE TELEVISION WITH TALL CABINETS TO SOFTEN ALL THAT TECHNOLOGY.

ABOVE LUSH VELVET DRAPERIES ON A U-SHAPE ROD CREATE THE ILLUSION OF A BAY WINDOW. OPPOSITE ANTIQUE SCHOOL LOCKERS SOLVE A STORAGE ISSUE IN THE ENTRYWAY; THEIR NARROW WIDTH IS IDEAL FOR THIS SMALL SPACE.

TROPICAL PARADISE

Bright striped fabric inspires this family room fiesta that's splashed with a juicy, lip-smacking palette of fresh, fruity colors.

Raspberry, lime, lemon, and tangerine. A list of ingredients for fruit salad? No, but it provided a recipe for a colorful redo of Janet's family room—a popular hangout that was worn out from use.

Fortunately, the generous space is loaded with architectural character, with two handsome columns framing a wall of windows that overlook a wonderful view of the garden. The bay between the columns wasn't well-used, however. I decided to put the space to work by tucking a built-in sofa between the columns. Cushions made from a fun striped fabric in bright colors inspired a warm, tropical palette for the room.

Because the windows are such assets, I didn't want to cover them with heavy draperies. Instead, light sheers hang from a rod installed above the window frame. They can be drawn across the window to filter bright morning light and at other times of day can be pulled back to take in the garden

BEFORE

view. Long striped panels with tasseled trim frame the sheers and soften the architecture. An overdoor valance hangs at the same height as the draperies to unify the windows and door.

This room has to serve multiple purposes, so I established activity zones for conversation and TV watching, homework and crafts, and dining. In the TV zone, a coat of white paint refreshed the existing built-in oak cabinetry. A new decorative shelf installed above the TV displays a few pieces from Janet's collection of china pigs. A new sofa in a sunny yellow plaid and a pair of chairs upholstered in raspberry fabric define an inviting place to curl up and relax.

The placement of the sofa forms a visual wall that separates this area from the zone for homework, crafts, and snacks. The centerpiece of this secondary zone is a new round table, chosen to mirror the round window and a rounded cutout in the wall. The circles create a satisfying symmetry.

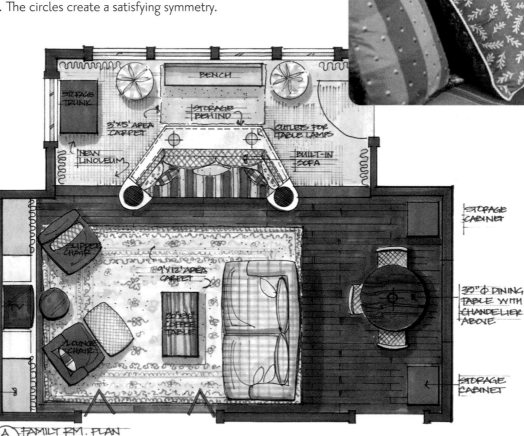

ABOVE THROW PILLOWS REPEAT HUES PULLED FROM THE STRIPED FABRIC—THE INSPIRATION FOR THIS ROOM'S COLOR PALETTE—AND MAKE THE BUILT-IN SOFA INVITING AND COMFORTABLE. OPPOSITE PAINTING THE OAK CABINETS WHITE GAVE THEM A FRESH START. YELLOW FABRIC PANELS CAN CLOSE TO CONCEAL CLUTTER.

MATCHING THE TABLE TO THE ARCHITECTURE CREATES A PLEASING REPETITION OF CIRCULAR FORMS AT THIS END OF THE ROOM.

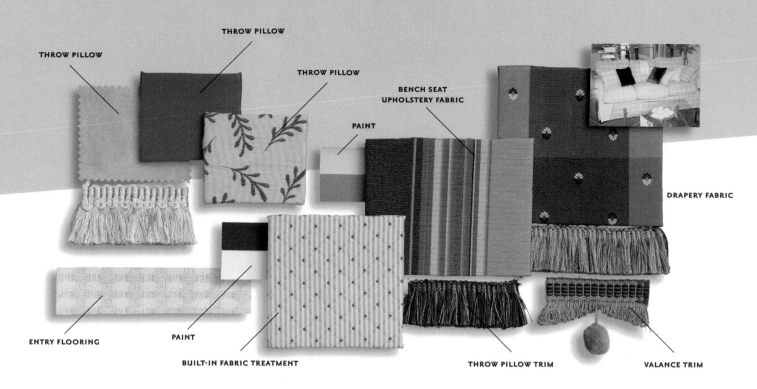

THROW PILLOW

THROW PILLOW

THROW PILLOW

BENCH SEAT
UPHOLSTERY FABRIC

PAINT

DRAPERY FABRIC

ENTRY FLOORING

PAINT

BUILT-IN FABRIC TREATMENT

THROW PILLOW TRIM

VALANCE TRIM

Although this room had plenty of natural light during the day, it was poorly lit at night. To remedy this situation, we used retrofit kits to transform the old recessed lights into 3-inch halogen fixtures. The lights can be directed to spotlight special areas and collections. A lantern-style sconce provides accent lighting. A country-inspired chandelier and tall table lamps behind the built-in sofa supply task lighting. Now Janet and her family can enjoy the juicy colors of their new tropical paradise day or night.

ABOVE OPEN SPACE BENEATH THE BUILT-IN SOFA ACCOMMODATES BASKETS FOR STORAGE. STEPS TO THE RIGHT OF THE BUILT-IN SOFA LEAD DOWN TO A SMALL FOYER WITH ACCESS TO THE BACK OF THE SOFA, WHERE MORE SHELVES AND HOOKS STORE THE KIDS' BELONGINGS. OPPOSITE JANET'S THREE CHILDREN HAVE LUNCH AT THE NEW ROUND TABLE AND ALSO USE IT FOR DOING HOMEWORK AND PROJECTS.

PAINT PERFECT

WHENEVER YOU DRESS WALLS IN RICH COLORS, SUCH AS THIS TROPICAL TANGERINE, PLAN ON ROLLING ON A NUMBER OF COATS TO ENSURE COMPLETE COVERAGE. IN SOME CASES, YOU'LL WANT TO START WITH PRIMER—ESPECIALLY IF YOU ARE COVERING A LIGHT TONE WITH DARK OR VICE VERSA. HAVE THE PAINT STORE TINT THE PRIMER WITH SOME OF YOUR WALL COLOR. TO ACHIEVE AN EVEN FINISH TONE, YOU MAY NEED TWO COATS OF COLOR—POSSIBLY THREE OR MORE—DEPENDING ON THE INTENSITY OF THE TOPCOAT COLOR AGAINST THE PRIMER COAT. DON'T SKIMP WITH THIS STEP—PAINT IS ONE OF THE LEAST EXPENSIVE DECORATING TOOLS AROUND.

BELOW This previously remodeled attic family room had no charm. OPPOSITE Club chairs and a table define a snacking/reading/game-playing zone. Flanking the sofa, carved-wood hippo heads hold copper buckets for stashing DVDs, books, and the remote control.

HOUSETOP HANGOUT

AN ATTIC BECOMES A HIP RETREAT FOR TWO PRETEEN BOYS AND THEIR FRIENDS, PROVING THAT STYLE AND FUN MAKE A WINNING TEAM.

WHAT PRETEEN WOULDN'T DO BACKFLIPS TO have his or her very own getaway? For most kids, the bedroom is the only space they can call their own. But if you have a bonus space, such as an attic, a basement, or a room over the garage, why not turn it into a preteen retreat? Make it a comfortable space for them to play, study, and hang out with friends, and you'll always know where your kids are.

That was the goal of this homeowner. Previous owners had finished the attic to use as a family room, and the current owner wanted to turn the space over to her two preteen boys to give them a place to do homework, play foosball, and watch TV. But the rough, white stucco walls and ceiling and gray industrial carpet looked impersonal and bland, and other than the foosball table, there was nothing much to draw the boys up there. On the good side, the room had lots of big windows, which let in plenty of light and air.

BEFORE

To determine how best to design the space, I asked Mom and the boys how they wanted to use the room. The boys voted for a place to play foosball and watch TV. Mom requested a place for them to study. So I designed one area around the foosball table, with a built-in snack bar and mini refrigerator and a window

HARD-WEARING DENIM DRESSES UP THE CHAIRS IN MASCULINE STYLE AND STANDS UP TO WHATEVER THE BOYS DISH OUT.

bench for spectators. For watching TV and DVDs, a comfy slipcovered sofa anchors a new seating area that includes club chairs, floor pillows, and beanbag chairs. For the homework station, a new built-in desk and shelves turn an awkward window area into a functional study spot.

To give the attic retreat guy-friendly personality, I chose natural, masculine materials and colors. Wheat-color berber carpet replaced the old carpeting, offering softness underfoot as well as texture that hides minor accidents. A caramel color on the walls warms up the rooms but reflects light well. Denim upholstery, cotton duck, and dark wood and leather accents round out the palette of textures and colors.

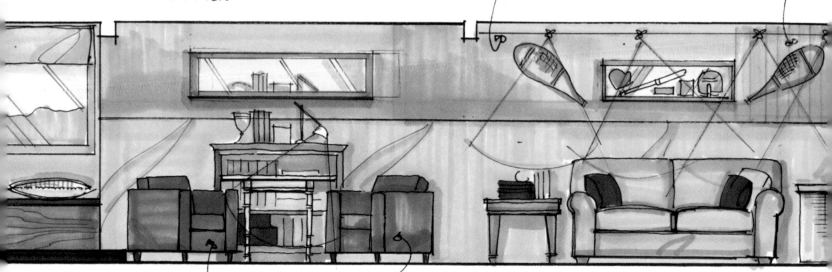

EXISTING BENCH CLAD WITH WOOD ON TOP & FACE. NEW SEAT CUSHIONS

CABLE LIGHTING SYSTEM

SPORTS PARAPHERNALIA ON ANGLED CEILING

BOOKSHELF, TABLE AND LOUNGE CHAIRS AS LIBRARY

As to lighting, you know my mantra—the right lights are key to bringing a room to life. For one wall in the game area, I chose a halogen fixture as accent lighting. But I have to admit, I chose it not because it was functional but because it was fun. The swoopy metal arm and funny little figures holding the lamps were just plain cool! Wall sconces with shades illuminate the study area, and mirrors mounted on the angled ceiling help bounce more light into the rooms.

With their hockey trophies on display and sporting equipment on the walls, the boys can claim this space as their own housetop retreat.

AFFORDABLE DESK

MOM REQUESTED A HOMEWORK AREA (FUNNY HOW THE BOYS NEVER ASKED FOR THIS!) WITH PROPER LIGHTING AND AMPLE WORK SURFACE SO THE BOYS COULD SPREAD OUT HOMEWORK, STUDY WITH FRIENDS, AND WORK AT THE COMPUTER. WITH A STRICT BUDGET IN MIND, WE BUILT IN SIMPLE MAPLE STORAGE SHELVES AND A TWO-TIERED COMPUTER DESK. TWO STAIN COLORS—A NATURAL TONE AND A DARK WALNUT—GIVE THE WOODWORK DIMENSION AND INTEREST. THIS IS A GREAT TECHNIQUE FOR GETTING A QUALITY, HIGH-DOLLAR LOOK WITHOUT SPENDING A LOT OF MONEY.

ABOVE RIGHT THE SNACK BAR, WITH ITS MINI REFRIGERATOR, IS CONVENIENTLY LOCATED NEAR THE FOOSBALL TABLE. THE HALOGEN LIGHT FIXTURE WAS TOO FUN TO RESIST. OPPOSITE USING STRAIGHT CUTS AND MAPLE LUMBER, WE BUILT A DESK UNIT AROUND ONE LARGE WINDOW. LEATHER OTTOMANS ARE EASY TO MOVE TO OTHER PARTS OF THE ROOM IF THE BOYS HAVE MANY FRIENDS OVER AND NEED MORE SEATING IN FRONT OF THE TV OR AROUND THE FOOSBALL TABLE.

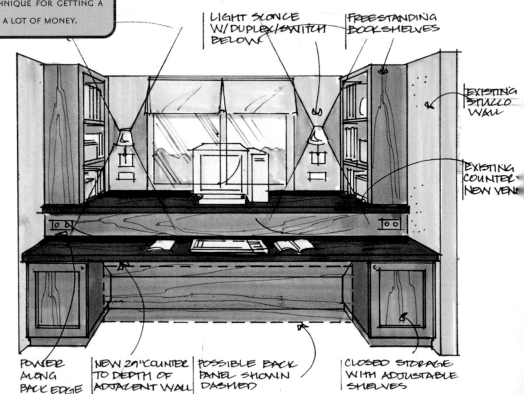

LIGHT SCONCE W/DUPLEX/SWITCH BELOW

FREESTANDING BOOKSHELVES

EXISTING STUDIO WALL

EXISTING COUNTER NEW VENE

POWER ALONG BACK EDGE

NEW 27"COUNTER TO DEPTH OF ADJACENT WALL

POSSIBLE BACK PANEL SHOWN DASHED

CLOSED STORAGE WITH ADJUSTABLE SHELVES

DESIGN ESSENTIALS: DINE, GATHER, RELAX

WHEN A DINING ROOM, LIVING ROOM, AND FAMILY ROOM OFTEN ARE DESERTED, HERE'S HOW I TRANSFORM THEM INTO POPULAR DESTINATIONS.

① GOT A FLOP? DO THE FLIP.

When most people buy a home, they have an area that's already been labeled "the dining room." It looks like one, it smells like one, and so—by golly—they think this has to be one. Let's say, however, that you frequently entertain 10 guests in the dining room, but it barely will hold a table for six. So here you have these people squeezed around the dinner table—all with a lovely view of the adjacent spacious living room, which, by the way, is layered in cobwebs because it is never used. So why not consider flipping the function of these two spaces? Even if the larger space is the first room that people see when they enter your house, it can become a "wowie!" dining room and make a spectacular first impression. (Plus, it's all legal—I promise the cops won't show up!)

BEFORE

ABOVE AND RIGHT THIS FAMILY WANTED TO HOST GATHERINGS OF 30 TO 35 PEOPLE, SO WE FLIPPED THE USES OF THE ROOMS, RELOCATING THE DINING ROOM INTO THE FORMER LIVING ROOM.

To help you make the decision on whether to flip the functions of two rooms, think about how you live in your house and what size groups you want to host around a table. If you often entertain large groups and need the space to bring in additional tables to supplement the dining table, performing a room function flip-flop may be just what you need.

the living room, you can place "extra" chairs in the living room. Whenever you need additional seating in the dining room, the chairs easily relocate from the living room to the table and back again when you're done.

You also can place ottomans around your house and use them for extra seating. Ottomans on casters are easy to move around to wherever you need them.

This same move-it-where-you-need-it approach works with additional tables. You can place dropleaf gateleg tables in rooms close to the dining room. When you need additional dining space, you can bring this extra table into the room. Because you've mixed things up, the extra table looks as though it belongs.

② MOTHER SAYS SUITES ARE BAD FOR YOU.

It's no secret that my signature style is to mix and contrast different styles and periods to keep things looking lively and livable, so you probably will never see me use a

BEFORE

matching suite of furniture in a dining room—unless, of course, I'm retaining the homeowners' existing set at their request or we're on a budget. (People tell me they love to buy these matching dining room suites because you get the sixth piece free.)

But besides getting a better look when you mix up furnishings, there are some practical reasons for my approach: By using different styles of chairs with a variety of fabrics that work in both the dining room and

③ TV, ANYONE?

If you're one of the lucky people who own a new, beautiful flat screen television, I'm here to tell you that you don't have to hide it. Hang it above the living room or family room fireplace if you want. Put it anywhere that provides easy viewing when your friends gather for food and the football game.

On the other hand, if you still own one of the less attractive

BEFORE

black boxes as I do, then let's work it into some basic cabinetry or a custom-built cabinetry unit to get it out of sight. One caveat: If the TV is bigger than you are, don't bother. It is the focal point of the room, and nothing is going to change that. Nevertheless, you can tame that high-tech look by flanking a giant television with attractive cabinetry and work in some beauty around the beast.

Here's a trick to stretch the budget: Purchase ready-made freestanding bookshelves that are unfinished (in the desired size) and position them on each side of the television. Secure the shelves to the wall (screw through the back of the shelves into the wall studs). Create a built-in look by edging the top and bottom of the shelves with crown molding or a simpler

BEFORE

profile molding, if you prefer. You also can bridge the gap between shelves by installing a fascia board between shelves and topping it with molding to match. Paint or stain your new shelving unit as desired.

LEFT To hold Nicole's television—dubbed the "boyfriend keeper"— I designed a stunning chocolate brown custom entertainment center. To take the focus off the television, the cabinet unit extends into a bench with a padded backrest. ABOVE I elevated Andrew and Lisa's cool television to focal-point status.

TRICK OF THE TRADE

PINA AND HELDER'S DINING ROOM, *right,* ILLUSTRATES A NEAT, MONEY-SAVING ARCHITECTURAL STRATEGY. SIMPLE BUILDER'S MOLDINGS WERE ALREADY IN PLACE SO RATHER THAN SPEND BIG BUCKS ON CUSTOM TRIM WORK, WE CREATED THE ILLUSION OF SOME. WE VISUALLY EXTENDED THE MOLDING BY TRIMMING WHAT WAS THERE WITH MATCHING PIECES—INSTALLED PARALLEL TO THE EXISTING TRIM BUT SEVERAL INCHES APART. PAINTING THE MOLDINGS AND THE SPACE BETWEEN THEM GLOSSY WHITE TRICKS THE EYE INTO BELIEVING IT IS ONE SUBSTANTIAL PIECE OF MOLDING.

more intimate and welcoming feeling.

You could have a television-viewing zone, for example, in one part of the room, using a sectional around the television. In  another part of the room, put down a large area rug and position the dining table on top of it. Then use these and other furnishings to define a game area for the kids. For additional definition and to obscure clutter, position folding freestanding screens wherever you need them or hang fabric panels to extend from the ceiling to the floor. The secret is to let the overall space flow but to deploy the furniture to define the purpose of the zone.

LEFT AND ABOVE THE FIREPLACE WAS A NATURAL ANCHOR FOR THE CONVERSATION ZONE IN NICOLE'S LIVING/DINING ROOM. WE ADDED MORE COMFORTABLE FURNITURE, LIGHTING, AND ACCESSORIES TO ENHANCE ITS FUNCTION. FURNITURE ALSO DEFINES THE ZONES FOR DINING AND FOR TELEVISION VIEWING AND ENJOYING COCKTAILS (THE TELEVISION CABINET ON THE OPPOSITE PAGE).

④ ENTER THE ZONE

When your home features a large multipurpose space for living, gathering, and dining, people sometimes want to push furniture to the outside edges of the room. But you'll find life more organized and contained if you arrange furnishings and belongings in "zones." Arranging furniture in zones is also a much more attractive look and gives a room a

BEDROOMS
(FOR GROWN-UPS)

Kick off your shoes and put on your favorite slippers. These bedrooms will show you how to put some zip in the space where you get your Zs!

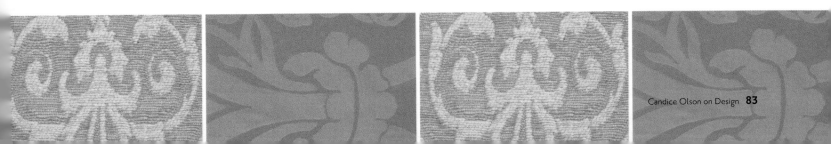

FASHION FORWARD

ONCE A FLASHBACK TO THE 1980s, THIS BEDROOM IS NOW DRESSED IN ELEGANT FABRICS, CLASSIC FURNISHINGS, AND TRANQUIL COLORS.

WHAT WERE WE THINKING IN THE '80S? TAKE THIS master bedroom in its previous life, for example. These pastel colors were trendy in 1982, but today they remind us of an Easter egg! The room's style was older than the owners' teenage girls, so it definitely was time for a fresh and fashionable makeover.

The rest of the house is bright and colorful, nothing like this pink-and-teal time capsule. After chatting with the owners, I learned that what they longed for was a quiet oasis that was stylish and serene. Mom wanted a place where she could relax and read, and Dad wanted to be able to watch television.

Creating the right mood started with color. Soft sage green on the walls and creamy white on the ceiling immediately brought the energy level lower so the room felt calmer and quieter. The cream-color broadloom carpet was in good shape, so we left it in place, but layering the carpet with an

BEFORE

Aubusson-style needlepoint area rug introduced soft green and faded-salmon accents on the floor. For the headboard, bedding, window treatments, and upholstered benches, I chose a mix of prints, stripes, and plaids in a muted, low-contrast palette of sage, mocha, and caramel. Texture counts too: The satiny sheen

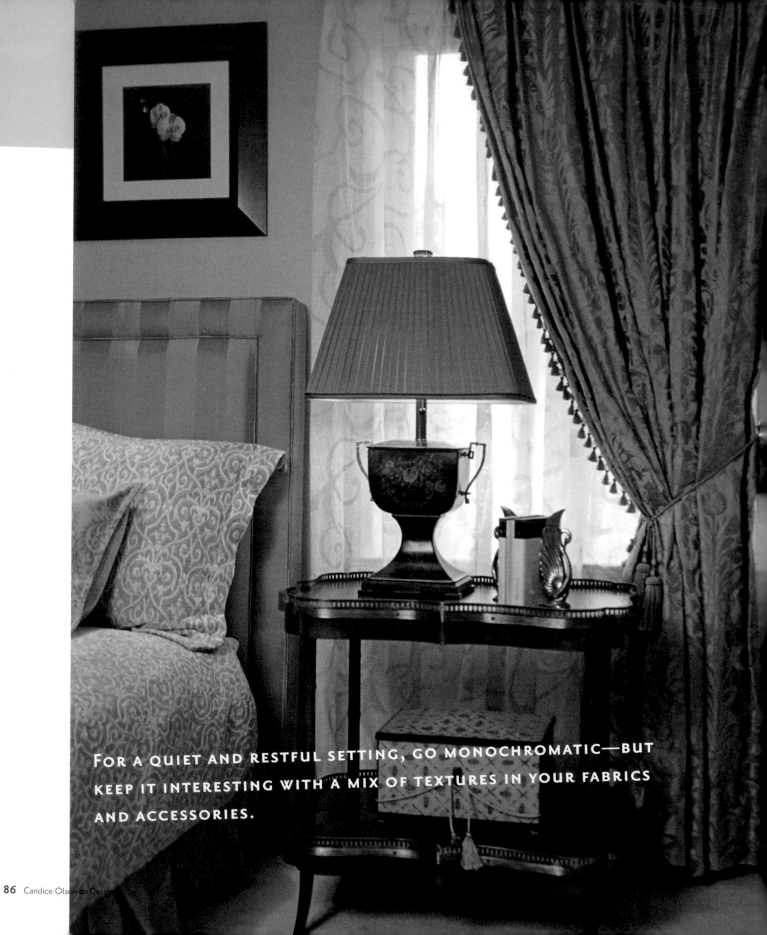

For a quiet and restful setting, go monochromatic—but keep it interesting with a mix of textures in your fabrics and accessories.

OPPOSITE **ALTHOUGH THE COLORS ARE UNDERSTATED, PATTERNS IN THE DRAPERIES, SHEERS, BED LINENS, AND HEADBOARD OFFER A FEAST OF TEXTURE.** RIGHT **I LOVE THE CONTRAST OF MATTE AND SHINY SURFACES—THAT'S WHAT MAKES THE MOCHA AND SAGE HEADBOARD FABRIC REALLY POP.**

of the drapery fabric and headboard stripe gives the room instant elegance.

The old furniture had to go—there was no saving that headboard, and the matching suite of campaign-furniture side tables and dresser screamed 1980s redux. We replaced it with a stylish and eclectic mix of both new and antique furniture. Flanking the bed with mismatched bedside tables—a two-tier table on one side and a small chest on the other—creates a sophisticated, evolved-over-time look. A large walnut armoire (not shown) houses the TV near the bed for Dad's viewing comfort.

CHEST OF DRAWERS
7"x20" x
1'2"h

82" x 55"y 9"
HEADBD.

FULL LENGTH DRAPERY PANELS ...SHEERS BEHIND ON DECORATIVE WOODEN ROD

TIER TABLE
30"x20"x27"H

A ELEVATION @ BED
3   1'2"="1'0"

HEADBOARD
UPHOLSTERY FABRIC

BEDDING

DRAPERY SHEERS

THROW PILLOW

CABINET PAINT

THROW PILLOW

PAINT

DRAPERY PANELS

ABOVE NEW GLASS SHELVING HELPED UPDATE THIS EXISTING BUILT-IN BOOKCASE. THE GLASS SHELVES ALSO ALLOW THE ILLUMINATION TO BRIGHTEN THIS SECTION OF THE DISPLAY CASE. OPPOSITE YOU ONLY NEED A SLIVER OF SPACE TO CARVE OUT A COMFY CORNER FOR READING. THIS INVITING SPOT COMES TOGETHER WITH AN UPHOLSTERED CHAIR AND A SMALL SIDE TABLE.

To accommodate Mom's wish for a reading nook, I tucked an overstuffed reading chair, table lamp, and a side table in one corner. In the adjacent corner, a built-in cabinet and shelves received a facelift with fresh paint, new glass shelves, and recessed spotlights. Replacing two of the veneer shelves with glass and installing lights gives this piece new sparkle and makes it a showcase for glass pieces, art, and photos.

Today the once-trendy 1980s look is all but a historical footnote. Dressed in restrained colors and elegant textures, the master bedroom is serene, sophisticated, and—dare we say it?—timeless.

BOOKCASE BEAUTIFICATION

IF YOU HAVE A STURDY BUILT-IN BOOKCASE OR CABINETRY IN THE BED-ROOM, LUCKY YOU! HERE ARE SOME MORE WAYS YOU CAN FRESHEN THESE STORAGE AND DISPLAY WORKHORSES:

• BRIGHTEN DARK OR OAK-STAINED BUILT-INS WITH PAINT. LIGHTLY SAND THE SURFACES, WIPE AWAY RESIDUE WITH A TACK CLOTH, AND BRUSH ON PRIMER. ONCE DRY, BRUSH ON ONE OR MORE COATS OF HIGH-QUALITY, ULTRADURABLE LATEX CABINET PAINT. (YOUR PAINT DEALER CAN HELP YOU CHOOSE.)

• IF YOUR BOOKCASE ALSO FEATURES CABINET DOORS, LIKE THIS ONE, REPLACE DATED HARDWARE WITH NEW KNOBS, PULLS, AND HINGES.

BEST FOR LAST

AN ATTIC MASTER BEDROOM IS THE LAST ROOM IN THE HOUSE TO RECEIVE AN UPDATED PERSONALITY, BUT IT PROVES TO BE WORTH THE WAIT.

THE MASTER BEDROOM IS OFTEN THE LAST ROOM IN the house to be renovated. Blake, Sharon, and their three children spent countless hours restoring their century-old Victorian home to its original glory: The living room, dining room, and the children's rooms underwent complete refurbishing. But the couple's attic bedroom, at the top of the house and last on the list, remained an eyesore. Angled ceilings and walls had been painstakingly covered in blue and white stripe wallpaper, which emphasized the chopped-up feeling of the space. Bold floral curtains overpowered one section of the room, while green carpeting and mismatched bedding and furniture took the color scheme off in a different (and disjointed) direction from the wallcovering and draperies.

Although the rest of the house is traditional, I decided that a contemporary redo would work well here because the attic is visually separate from the rest of the house. We didn't need to

BEFORE

worry about being historically accurate or continuing any themes from downstairs.

The first step was to strip the stripes off those walls. Painting all surfaces a soft cream color unified the jutting angles, and once my new lighting plan was in place, the cream color would actually

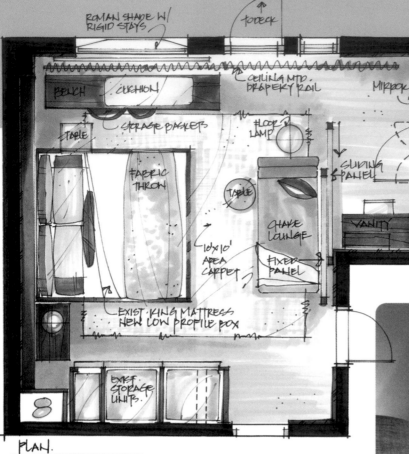

ROMAN SHADE W/ RIGID STAYS

TO DECK

BENCH

CUSHION

CEILING MTD. DRAPERY RAIL

MIRROR

STORAGE BASKETS

TABLE

FLOOR LAMP

FABRIC THROW

TABLE

SLIDING PANEL

CHAISE LOUNGE

VANITY

10'x10' AREA CARPET

FIXED PANEL

EXIST. KING MATTRESS NEW LOW PROFILE BOX

8

EXIST. STORAGE UNITS.

PLAN.
1/2" = 1'-0"

BELOW Mirror-wrapped night tables flank the bed for a touch of glamour. The tables are mounted on the wall so they float above the floor, increasing the room's perceived space. OPPOSITE A beautiful bay window alcove becomes an intimate area for conversation and reading.

give those angles a sculptural quality. Mushroom-color carpeting anchored the room with a warm, neutral hue.

With this soothing backdrop in place, I chose furnishings, fabrics, and accessories in a range of neutrals, with punches of toasty color for accents. Dark neutrals—brown, dark taupe, and black—ground the scheme and give it weight. Rust, cinnamon, and gold accents add warmth, while large doses of pale taupe, cream, and off-white keep the overall look on the light side.

An array of textures, including puckered silk, mohair, and raffia, enrich the sophisticated effect of the neutral colors. They also introduce a feeling of luxury. What could be yummier, after all, than leaning against a padded, mohair-upholstered

SHIMMERY FABRICS, CONTEMPORARY ARTWORK, AND SHAPELY CERAMICS GIVE THIS MASTER BEDROOM A MODERN WAKE-UP CALL.

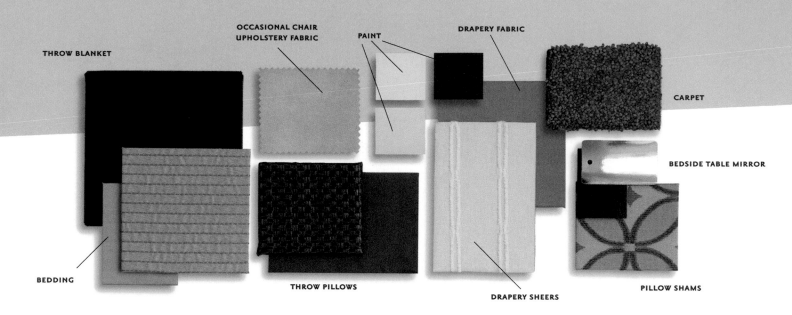

THROW BLANKET

OCCASIONAL CHAIR UPHOLSTERY FABRIC

PAINT

DRAPERY FABRIC

CARPET

BEDSIDE TABLE MIRROR

BEDDING

THROW PILLOWS

DRAPERY SHEERS

PILLOW SHAMS

ABOVE IRIDESCENT CURTAIN PANELS SHIMMER UNDER THE RECESSED LIGHTING. PAIRED WITH PRINTED SHEERS, THEY EMPHASIZE THE SPACE OF THE BAY. ABOVE RIGHT CANDLES LIGHT THIS CHANDELIER TO PROVIDE A ROMANTIC GLOW. OPPOSITE AN AWKWARD SPACE BENEATH THE WINDOWS IS JUST RIGHT FOR A SMALL HOME OFFICE AREA. NEAT ROMAN SHADES IN SHIMMERY FABRIC DRESS THE WINDOWS WITH TAILORED ELEGANCE.

headboard to read in bed? A quilted taupe silk coverlet, embroidered pillow shams, and plump silky pillows add to the tactile appeal.

Elegant fabrics dress the bay window too. Stationary panels in iridescent blue-gold-green form shimmering columns flanking sheer panels that control light and provide privacy. With two comfy chairs and a candlelit chandelier, this area becomes a cozy spot for relaxing.

New lighting brought out the sculptural quality of the space, with recessed halogen lights in the ceiling, pharmacy lamps behind the chairs, and table lamps beside the bed.

With its elegant finishes, luxurious lighting and linens, and contemporary furniture and flourishes, this bedroom is now a high-style retreat for Sharon and Blake—a final home renovation that surely was worth the wait.

VA-VA-VOOM BEDROOM

HERE'S ONE OF THE MORE WONDERFUL GIFTS A COUPLE COULD GIVE THEM-

SELVES: A COCOONLIKE RETREAT LAVISHED IN RICH BROWN AND BLUE.

SOME COUPLES GO OUT FOR DINNER TO CELEBRATE
an anniversary, but Janet and Wayne opted for something more lasting: They decided to commemorate 10
years of marriage by giving themselves a new master
bedroom retreat.

There wasn't anything memorable about the couple's
sparsely furnished bedroom: White walls, white bedding,
and white paper blinds made this space the definition of
stark and sterile. To turn it into the epitome of drama and
romance, I decided to take the color palette in the opposite
direction: deep bronze, dark blue, and dark chocolate, with
ice-blue accents. This new room would be an enveloping, restful cocoon far from the hectic rush of their daily lives.

The conversion began with deep lagoon blue on the walls.
Fabrics on the bed and at the windows balance the blue with
warm bronze. To give the room a show-stopping focal point, I
designed a custom-made headboard that dominates one wall.

BEFORE

Thickly upholstered in tufted bronze fabric, it includes built-in
sconces that cast a romantic glow perfect for reading in bed. To
pull the color scheme together, a bronze, brown, and blue stripe
fabric skirts the bed and trims the bedcover, draperies, and tailored valance.

TO KEEP A DRAMATICALLY DARK COLOR SCHEME FROM FEELING OVERPOWERING, INTRODUCE LIGHT-COLOR ACCENTS, FURNITURE, AND FLOORING.

With reading lights incorporated into the headboard, Wayne and Janet could dispense with the usual bedside tables. Instead, I designed a dramatic floating shelf and tall mirror for each side of the bed. The shelves provide a spot for family photos or an alarm clock, and the mirrors add sparkle and the illusion of greater space. Boxes in a dark brown finish stack under the shelves to store reading material and other bedside necessities.

To balance the visual weight of the bed and to provide a place for the TV, I brought in a dark wood armoire and placed it on the wall opposite the headboard. A black leather bench at the

WAYNE & JANET'S BEDROOM · ELEV @ HEADBD.

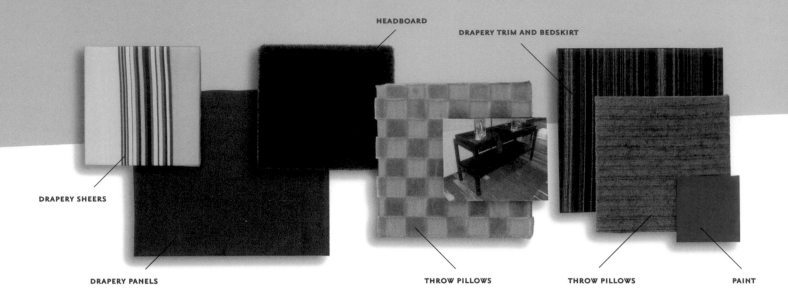

DRAPERY SHEERS

HEADBOARD

DRAPERY TRIM AND BEDSKIRT

DRAPERY PANELS

THROW PILLOWS

THROW PILLOWS

PAINT

foot of the bed provides a place to sit while dressing.

At the windows, a lush multilayered treatment of sheers, side panels, and a valance offers the option of filtering light or drawing the draperies for complete privacy. Recessed lighting in the ceiling washes the draperies with pools of light. A shapely chandelier with strands of light-reflecting crystal beads hangs above the bed for a fun touch of sparkle in an otherwise dramatically dark room.

Now an elegant and romantic refuge, this master bedroom boasts a fresh, new look to help Janet and Wayne stylishly kick off their next 10 years of wedded bliss.

BALANCING ACT

BEDROOMS REQUIRE A BIT OF A BALANCING ACT WHEN IT COMES TO SCALE. LOOK AT YOUR BED, AND YOU'LL SEE THAT IT INTRODUCES A LARGE HORIZONTAL SURFACE TO THE SPACE. YOUR BED DESERVES FOCAL-POINT ATTENTION, BUT YOU DON'T WANT IT TO STEAL ALL THE GLORY. THEN CONSIDER THE BED ALONG WITH THE CEILING, THE FLOOR, AND SIDE TABLES—A WHOLE LOT OF HORIZONTAL SURFACES. THAT'S WHY I FLIP SOME OF THAT EXPANSE TO THE VERTICAL SO THAT THE ATTENTION IS EVENED OUT. IN JANET AND WAYNE'S BEDROOM, THE EXTRA-TALL HEADBOARD, THE ARMOIRE, AND THE PLUSH WINDOW TREATMENTS DO THE TRICK.

ABOVE DARK CHOCOLATE SUITCASE-STYLE BOXES PROVIDE MORE STORAGE THAN THE AVERAGE NIGHTSTAND. THE FLOATING SHELF AND MIRROR FRAME ARE IN THE SAME DARK WOOD AS THE ARMOIRE, SO ALL THE WOOD TONES WORK TOGETHER. OPPOSITE A LIGHT-COLOR CARPET AND CHAIR AND CRISP WHITE BASEBOARDS PROVIDE VISUAL RELIEF FROM THE DARK COLORS. THE STRIPED RUG OVER THE CARPET BRINGS THE COLOR THEME TO THE FLOOR TO ROUND OUT THE DESIGN.

GRACIOUSLY GROWN-UP

CHILDREN ARE A DELIGHT, BUT EVERY PARENT DESERVES AN ATTRACTIVE ADULT RETREAT DEDICATED TO RELAXING AND RENEWING.

KELLY AND MIKE'S BEDROOM WAS SUFFERING from a bad case of the blahs: bland color on the walls and floor, ho-hum bedding, and mismatched furniture, all reflected in floor-to-ceiling mirrored closet doors. "Accessories" consisted of toys and clutter belonging to their 1-year-old son, Jacob.

While they could overlook the kid stuff, Kelly and Mike really wanted the master bedroom to become a space to call their own—a room that would be stylish, adult, and relaxing. They leaned toward a modern look but didn't want the room to feel sterile or cold. The solution? Combine dark woods and clean lines that suggest an Asian inspiration with upholstered pieces in traditional shapes to create a "soft modern" style.

I started with the walls. To anchor the room with a major focal point, I turned one wall into the headboard, covering the surface from floor to ceiling with rough-hewn walnut-stained

BEFORE

wood flooring. The wall includes a ledge for artwork and accessories. A new platform bed with a dark-stained wood base is centered on this wall, flanked by simple cubes for bedside tables.

Instead of tearing out the closet and rebuilding it, we gave its mirrored doors a facelift. Wood replaces the brass valance, the

brass trim was painted silver, and we applied a frosted treatment in horizontal stripes to break up the expanse of reflective surface.

The remaining walls, trim, and doors were painted a soft putty color to create a restful (but not bland) environment. Truffle-color carpet covers the floor, and putty-hued linen sheers dress the windows, creating a light neutral envelope that balances the visual weight of the bed and headboard wall. For the bed, I chose simple light-color bedding in keeping with a modern aesthetic. A striped throw and pillow shams and decorative pillows brighten the neutral scheme with touches of paprika and mustard-gold.

WEST ELEVATION

FIFTEEN FEET OF LINEN SHEERS ALONG ONE ROD
FORM A FLOWING FABRIC EXTRAVAGANZA.

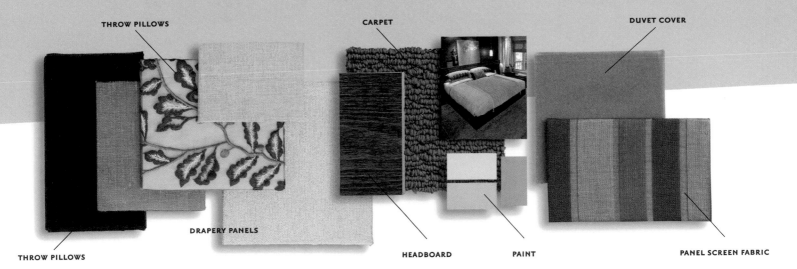

THROW PILLOWS

CARPET

DUVET COVER

DRAPERY PANELS

THROW PILLOWS

HEADBOARD

PAINT

PANEL SCREEN FABRIC

To provide ambience, we installed small, low-voltage halogen lights in the ceiling. For bedtime reading, two contemporary pendant lamps hang from the ceiling over the bedside tables.

On the wall opposite the bed, I created a dressing area for Kelly and Mike. Translucent panels of fabric (the same stripe that accents the pillow shams) screen this area from a chaise longue and the bed. Hanging from a rod mounted inside a shallow frame on the ceiling, the panels slide across the width of the room for privacy.

To put the finishing touches on this adult retreat, I chose Asian-influenced accessories, including sleek pottery, a vase of bamboo, and a painting of cherry blossoms. Now Kelly and Mike have a chic retreat that's big on comfort and style.

DIVIDE AND CONQUER

I CREATED A COZY, PRIVATE DRESSING NOOK WITHIN THIS MASTER BEDROOM USING TRANSLUCENT FABRIC AS A DIVIDER. WHEN THE DRESSING AREA ISN'T IN USE, THE FABRIC CAN SLIDE BEHIND A NEW CHAISE. IN LIEU OF A FABRIC DIVIDER, CONSIDER THESE ALTERNATIVES:

• A FREESTANDING FOLDING SCREEN. A WOOD SCREEN CAN BE STAINED OR PAINTED TO MATCH YOUR ROOM. YOU ALSO CAN CONSTRUCT A SCREEN AS A SERIES OF FRAMES TO HOLD COMPLEMENTARY FABRICS.

• A TWO-SIDED BOOKCASE CAN SERVE AS DISPLAY SPACE ON THE BEDROOM SIDE AND HOLD CLOTHING AND OTHER ITEMS ON THE OTHER SIDE.

OPPOSITE BEHIND THE FABRIC PANEL, A VANITY TABLE AND CHAIR FORM A STYLISH AND PRIVATE DRESSING NOOK. ABOVE A LOW BENCH OFFERS DISPLAY SPACE ON TOP BUT ALSO CAN SERVE AS A SPOT TO SIT. UNDERNEATH, BASKETS MAKE ATTRACTIVE STORAGE FOR BOOKS AND EXTRA BLANKETS.

DESIGN ESSENTIALS: ADULT BEDROOMS

HERE ARE SOME OF THE FUNDAMENTALS I DEPEND ON TO BEAUTIFY A BOUDOIR. YOU CAN USE THEM TO AWAKEN YOUR OWN SLEEPING BEAUTY.

① MIX UP FURNISHINGS

A matching suite of bedroom furniture is static—about as homey as a hotel room—and doesn't grow with you. When you mix up the styles and finishes of the pieces, your bedroom will feel more natural, personal, and inviting. Plus, this philosophy of variety in furnishings lets you easily add new pieces throughout the years.

I often mix and match various furnishings—one bedside table might be ornate gilded wood and one a little more traditional dark wood piece. The main concern in this case is that the tables should be the same height.

When you purchase a variety of furnishings, create a thread of continuity by including a similarly finished item elsewhere in the room, such as a gilt-framed mirror and a dark finished chair to go with the bedside tables.

ABOVE AND RIGHT PATTY AND ALLAN NEEDED A COHESIVE LOOK FOR THEIR BEDROOM. WHITE PROVIDES UNITY AMONG THE VARIOUS STORAGE AND SEATING PIECES THAT I BROUGHT IN TO BUST THE CLUTTER AND ADD COMFORT. WHITE LEATHER CUBES EASE THE TRANSITION AT THE FOOT OF THE BED, PROVIDING A STREAMLINED FINISH THAT'S FUNCTIONAL TOO.

I tend to avoid beds with footboards, but I do like to achieve a transition from the foot of the bed to the floor. This can be accomplished with ottomans or a bench—either of which should span most of the width of the bed. A bench in the bedroom is practical and pretty: Use it to sit and put on shoes or use it as a landing pad for books or a tray of tea in the morning.

LEFT AND BELOW LEFT MARNA AND BERNIE HAD ALREADY PAINTED THEIR BEDROOM A TRANQUIL SHADE OF WATERY GREEN, BUT THE LACK OF COLOR, PATTERN, AND TEXTURE LEFT THE SPACE MORE HO-HUM THAN RESTFUL. I INTRODUCED IRRESISTIBLE LUXURY BY LAYERING THE ROOM WITH A COMBINATION OF SILKS, CHENILLES, AND WASHABLE VELVETS.

③ COLOR YOUR WORLD

When it comes to selecting a color palette, let your heart and home guide you. Here's what I mean: If my clients are after a lot of drama, then I look for relatively deep tones. If, however, they desire a quiet, restful, and relaxing retreat, I go for lighter, more neutral colors and then play up texture to add interest. Many times, the choices also depend on the direction the room is facing. If the room receives little natural light, I don't try to fight it; I work with the low light and make the room moody and dramatic. If it is a sunny bedroom, then that dictates my choices and I can go with a lighter color palette.

② FINESSE WITH FABRICS

Decide from the outset whether you require fabrics that are as practical as they are pretty. Do you want washable fabric? If so, you may have to limit your use of rich, luxurious velvets or brocades. The good news is that I never sacrifice the look, and you don't have to either. There are wonderful polyester blends available (for instance, faux suedes have a comfortable, textural quality and are washable). Do you love a fabric that requires special care? Use it as a coverlet to lay across the foot of the bed. For contrast, I look for an eclectic mix of textures—maybe chenille and velvet paired with high-sheen satin or polished silk. Contrast is a big thing: old with new and rough with sleek. I might pair something heavily patterned with a solid or more subtle pattern. It is those layers of contrasting pattern and texture that create the overall interest.

BEFORE

4 DRESS THE ROOM

Window treatments offer a great opportunity to play up a vertical elevation and balance the horizontal expanse of the bed. (See "Balancing Act" on page 100.) Bedroom windows are usually very undersized, so I try to make these dinky openings appear larger. When space allows, I'll extend the treatments 2 to 3 feet on each side of the window to create the illusion of more expansive architecture.

Windows can also be quite low, so I can also trick the eye into seeing a taller window by extending a treatment to the ceiling. Though bedroom window treatments don't have to be totally practical—

they can be a little more "Liberace!"—you do want them to be functional. If you need a completely dark room to sleep in, use an underlayer, such as blackout blinds, to control light. You can soften these utilitarian blinds with an overlayer of floor-to-ceiling sheers, and then add luxurious side panels. These are often the ultimate prop because they don't have to be operable. Keep in mind that if your window faces south, natural materials can deteriorate in the sun. Cottons, silks, and linens, for example, need to be lined to prevent bleaching. This also holds true for dark-tone fabrics.

Accessories are another great way to dress up your bedroom. Because the bedroom is such a personal space, it is a great place for reflecting on memories and experiences. That's why I often accessorize by hunting around the house for special belongings. Photographs are especially appropriate for the bedroom. But remember, you can have too much of a good thing. Select your favorite photos and display just a few. If you have lots of favorites, rotate your display for variety.

ABOVE In this bedroom, I extended the window treatment to the ceiling line to create a grand, elegant look. LEFT I matted and framed a few prized photos for this bedroom redo and used them to dress up the closet doors. Adhesive-back hook-and-loop tape holds them in place.

tures provide a decorative function, they also boost ambient, or overall, lighting. You may need additional recessed fixtures or a central fixture to achieve a comfortable overall level of light.

You'll also need task lighting, such as beside the bed for reading. Whenever possible position the light so the bottom of the shade falls between your shoulders and eye level so you're not looking up into the lamp as you read. If you're short on space, use swing-arm lamps or sconces. In any case, bedside lighting should be individually controlled for the late-night reader.

⑤ LIGHT THE NIGHT

You can have luxurious fabrics, but unless the lighting is positioned to take advantage of the texture, it is money wasted. Silk, for instance, is dead without illumination. Position adjustable, recessed halogen fixtures about 12 to 16 inches away from the wall so the light shines on the fabric and brings it to life. The ring on the fixture lets you tilt the bulb so the light artfully sculpts the folds of the fabric. While these fix-

BEFORE

ABOVE AND TOP I REPLACED THE TRACK LIGHTING ABOVE ALEX'S BED WITH A CANOPY
FITTED WITH FIBER-OPTIC LIGHTS. AUSTRIAN CRYSTAL PENDANTS OVER THE LIGHTS
CREATE A LOOK THAT'S RESTFULLY REMINISCENT OF A TWINKLING NIGHT SKY. RIGHT
IN ROBYN'S GUEST BEDROOM, I SUSPENDED TWO SMALL CHANDELIERS ABOVE THE
BEDSIDE TABLES. THEY HANG LOW ENOUGH TO PROVIDE ADEQUATE TASK LIGHTING,
BUT ALLOW SPACE FOR BOOKS AND OTHER NIGHTSTAND BELONGINGS.

BEDROOMS
(FOR KIDS)

WHETHER YOUR CHILD IS AN INFANT OR A YOUNG ADULT MAKING A POST-COLLEGE PIT STOP BACK HOME, THE RIGHT BEDROOM CAN STIR UP SWEET DREAMS.

BEACH AHOY!

A fun and whimsical beach theme greets Michelle and Remi's baby boy. It's a look that adapts for any gender and lasts as a child grows.

Even though Michelle and Remi knew their first child would be a boy, they didn't want his room to be a typical baby-boy nursery. The empty spare room in their new townhouse was big enough to serve as their new son's bedroom from toddler to teen years, so they wanted a design that would be flexible enough to grow along with him.

The solution? A beach theme! The colors of sea and sand work perfectly for a boy, and the theme lends itself to a fun interpretation that can become more grown-up over time. Creating this environment started with the walls. I chose a light sand color for the bottom two-thirds of the walls to define the "shore." The top third was painted pale blue. With wispy clouds applied freehand, using a mix of four parts glaze to one part white paint, it became the sky. To highlight the crib area, I painted a pair of stylized lighthouses on the crib wall. For the sake of speed, I used an overhead projector to

BEFORE

trace the design onto the wall, but a simple geometric shape like this also could be drawn off using a level, ruler, and painter's tape. On the ceiling we installed a large painted compass—it will give the baby something interesting to look at, and it's sophisticated enough to be appropriate when he's older too.

OPPOSITE The handpainted lighthouses that flank the crib are more than decorative: Peg racks provide storage, and low-voltage lights serve as night-lights. RIGHT A handpainted wooden compass frames the ceiling light and creates an unusual focal point.

The paint colors for the wall murals and ceiling art—blue, sand, green, and coral-red—gave me my cues for the fabrics. I chose a mix of versatile stripes, solids, and prints, including a fun cabana-motif print that frames the two sets of windows.

The draperies help soften the architecture, but the real workhorses for the window treatments are the Roman shades. The multicolor stripe fabric is backed with blackout material to ensure darkness for a good night's sleep. This style of window treatment is neat and tailored, perfect for a boy's room, and the stripe has longevity. If he outgrows the cabana

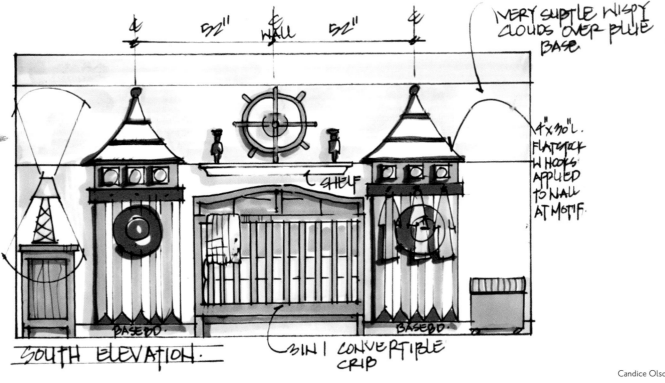

52" WALL 52"

VERY SUBTLE WISPY CLOUDS OVER BLUE BASE.

4"x 30"L. FLATSTOCK W HOOKS APPLIED TO WALL AT MOTIF.

SHELF

BASEBD.   BASEBD.

SOUTH ELEVATION.

3 IN 1 CONVERTIBLE CRIB

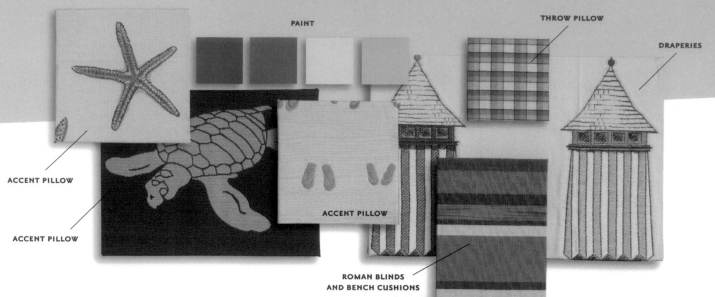

ACCENT PILLOW

ACCENT PILLOW

PAINT

ACCENT PILLOW

THROW PILLOW

DRAPERIES

ROMAN BLINDS
AND BENCH CUSHIONS

motif, the draperies easily can be replaced with solid-color ones or another nautical motif.

Michelle will be able to rock her son to sleep in the rocking chair that belonged to her mother. The rest of the furniture was purchased with an eye toward longevity (see below). A custom bench under the windows is also an adaptable piece, offering seating and storage.

We wrapped up this day at the beach with a few nautical splashes, including fish-shaped pillows, toy boats, and a life preserver. For Michelle and Remi's new son, every day will be a day at the beach!

FURNITURE TO LAST

HERE ARE SOME OF THE FURNITURE PIECES THAT I FOUND FOR THIS NURSERY THAT CAN REMAIN FUNCTIONAL AS THE BABY GROWS:

• A THREE-IN-ONE CRIB SERVES AS AN INFANT BED IN THE EARLY YEARS, CONVERTS INTO A TODDLER'S DAYBED, AND THEN SHIFTS INTO A FULL-SIZE BED AS THE CHILD GROWS UP.

• A NATURAL WOOD DRESSER SPORTS A CUSHION SO THE TOP CAN SERVE AS A CHANGING TABLE. THE CUSHION EASILY REMOVES ONCE BABY IS OUT OF THE DIAPER STAGE. THE DRESSER ALSO FEATURES AN OVERHEAD HUTCH FOR STORING NECESSITIES DURING EVERY STAGE.

ABOVE ACCESSORIES FROM LAMPS TO ARTWORK PLAY UP THE NAUTICAL THEME. OPPOSITE A ROCKING CHAIR THAT BELONGED TO MICHELLE'S MOTHER PAIRS WITH A SIDE TABLE TO CREATE A CORNER FOR ROCKING AND READING.

ADD DIMENSION AND COLOR WITH DRAPERIES, AND USE BLACKOUT BLINDS TO BLOCK SUNLIGHT.

FAIRY TALE TRANSFORMATION

This little girl's bedroom is a royal redo you can re-create for any princess who might reign in your household.

Once upon a time, Chantal and her family lived in a beautiful Victorian house. Although it was as grand as any castle, the nursery for the little princess, Michelle, needed an update: She was no longer an infant and was ready for a more grown-up space.

The room had wonderful architectural features but no color and no particular style. What a perfect opportunity to create a delightfully feminine environment! The look I had in mind would have a touch of whimsy to keep the room from feeling too sweet; it also would acknowledge Chantal's French-Canadian heritage, and it would suit the rest of the family's stately home.

Before adding any color, I first had to remedy some architectural quirks created by an earlier remodeling. The room apparently had been added onto the house, and two windows and a door had been turned into niches and a bookshelf. We covered those openings and smoothed the wall with drywall. I

BEFORE

then painted the room rose with hand-painted white "molding" that divides the walls into French-style faux panels. The result is elegant but not too serious.

Fabrics carry out a feminine color scheme of muted pink, rose, tangerine, and cream, with green accents. I chose rich, dressy

ELEGANT FABRICS AND AN ANTIQUE PAINTED BED CREATE A LUXURIOUS ENVIRONMENT THAT CAN TRANSITION FROM LITTLE GIRL TO TEEN.

fabrics—velvet, taffeta, and satin—with accents of organza and lace to establish an appropriately royal look. A beautiful cream-color satin embroidered with pink and tangerine flowers covers the bed and skirts a new built-in bench. For whimsical accents to lighten these elegant textiles, I chose a shaggy eyelash fabric for the bed skirt and pillow sham inserts and a pom-pom-studded sheer for cafe curtains at the windows.

Recessed lights wash down from the ceiling to make the fabrics sparkle, and antique wall sconces highlight the faux panels on each side of the bed. The truly royal lighting flourish, however is the custom chandelier over the bed, a French-style confection of roses, pearls, and crystal drops.

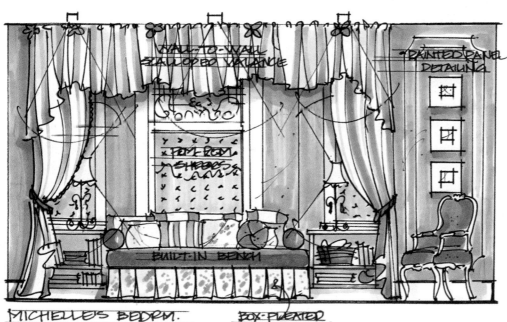

OPPOSITE A FEMININE GARDEN OF PINK FLOWERS BLOOMS ON THE BED LINENS, THE PILLOWS, AND EVEN THE HEADBOARD. ABOVE THE MARBLE TOP ON THIS ANTIQUE DRESSER SUGGESTS THE PIECE ORIGINALLY SERVED AS A WASHSTAND WITH A BOWL AND PITCHER FOR WASHING UP.

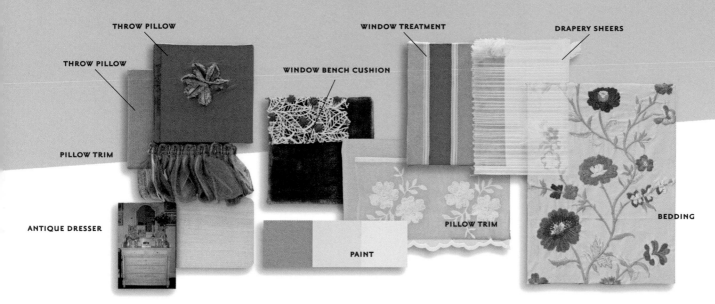

THROW PILLOW

THROW PILLOW

WINDOW TREATMENT

DRAPERY SHEERS

WINDOW BENCH CUSHION

PILLOW TRIM

ANTIQUE DRESSER

PAINT

PILLOW TRIM

BEDDING

A painted bed and dresser, both antiques, were obvious choices for furnishings. They are classic pieces that work for a young girl but will also suit her as a teen. For a bedside table, I found a French provincial chest that is new but works with the old pieces. A built-in bench tucked into the bay window provides extra seating for friends. I flanked it with matching side tables to give Michelle space for storage and display. Lustrous floor-length draperies and a deep valance hang just outside the bay on a straight rod installed at the ceiling. This emphasizes the bay window area as a cozy, semienclosed nook.

With the redo complete, Michelle has a bedroom that will always be perfect for a princess.

PAINTED FURNITURE

PAINTED FURNITURE WAS POPULAR IN THE 18TH AND 19TH CENTURIES IN NORTH AMERICA AND EUROPE AND CONTINUES TO INSPIRE REPRODUCTIONS. IF YOU'RE SHOPPING FOR ANTIQUE PAINTED FURNITURE, LOOK FOR ITEMS WITH THE PAINT INTACT; AVOID PIECES WITH FLAKING OR CHIPPING PAINT, ESPECIALLY FOR USE IN HOMES WITH SMALL CHILDREN. TO CREATE YOUR OWN PAINTED FURNITURE, USE EGGSHELL-FINISH INTERIOR PAINT FOR THE BASE COAT. APPLY DESIGNS WITH STENCILS OR DECOUPAGE, THEN SOFTEN AND "ANTIQUE" THE FINISH WITH A MIXTURE OF GLAZE AND PAINT.

OPPOSITE MATCHING SIDE TABLES HOLD BACK LUXURIOUS DRAPERIES THAT FRAME THE BAY WINDOW AND CREATE A FEELING OF ENCLOSURE. SHEER CAFE CURTAINS FILTER LIGHT BELOW THE LEADED-GLASS WINDOWS. ABOVE THE DRESSER IS NOT AGE-SPECIFIC, AND THE CHILD-SIZE FRENCH-STYLE FOLDING SCREEN IS SO CUTE THAT MICHELLE SURELY CAN FIND A DECORATIVE PURPOSE FOR IT WHEN SHE'S OLDER.

SIBLING SATISFACTION

BOLD FIRE ENGINE RED CAPTURES THE EXCITEMENT OF BEING YOUNG AND FRESH OUT OF COLLEGE AND HAVING THE WORLD AT YOUR FEET.

AFTER GRADUATING FROM COLLEGE, SISTERS Jennifer and Talia returned home to live. They'd shared a bedroom all their lives and figured they could pick up where they left off. Not so!

Besides lacking storage space, the bedroom was dated-looking, with worn green carpeting, blue walls, and old plaid bedspreads. These two young women were ready for something hip, a look that captured who they are now. And they wanted the elements to be portable so they could take them with them when they move out.

I decided to treat the room like a mini apartment, with different zones for sleeping and relaxing with friends. To create enough space for two twin beds in the sleep zone, we tore out the old closet (new storage units in the lounge area take over the closet function). Then, to give the room new personality, we painted the walls and ceiling with bold fire-engine red. I felt red best captured the excitement and new

BEFORE

possibilities awaiting the girls. White porch paint refreshed the worn hardwood flooring and, along with white woodwork, offered visual relief from the intense hue.

One challenge with a dark, strong color like red is that it absorbs light. To compensate for this, I chose halogen track

IN A SMALL ROOM, OPT FOR TAILORED WINDOW TREATMENTS THAT FIT INTO THE WINDOW FRAME. THEY'LL TAKE UP LESS SPACE VISUALLY.

lighting for both areas and added wall-mounted lamps in the lounge area and table lamps beside the bed. Light-reflecting surfaces such as a white shag rug, white sofa, and silver metallic Roman shades at the windows help amplify the effect of the lighting.

In the bedroom area, I chose bedding in shades of red, orange, and purple to blend with the walls. Continuous color enlarges the sense of space in a room because the eye finds no place to rest. A black dresser and a large poster in black, red, and white anchor the room visually.

In the lounge area, tall white storage cabinets provide space for clothing and shoes and can go with the young women when they move. The radiator ran along the wall between the cabinets

SILVER METALLIC ROMAN BLINDS

CUSTOM BEDSPREAD & BEDSKIRT

(A/3) ELEVATION @ WINDOW
JEN & TALIA'S BEDRM.

NEW FRONT WOOD DRESSER COVERS RADIATOR BEHIND

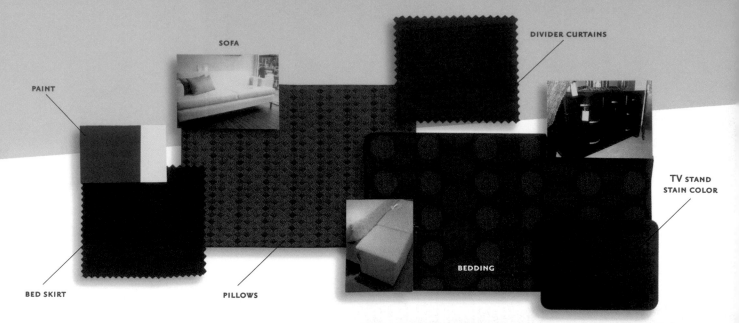

PAINT

SOFA

DIVIDER CURTAINS

TV STAND STAIN COLOR

BED SKIRT

PILLOWS

BEDDING

so I topped it with a custom shelf, then slipped an apartment-size white sofa between the cabinets. On the opposite wall I placed a simple ebony-stained table to hold the TV. Upholstered ottomans slip underneath and can slide out if the sisters need more seating or want to put their feet up. White wall-mounted shelves above the table provide plenty of space for display and will be easy to take down and transfer to an apartment.

This dramatic makeover gives the young women a hip new place to call home for now. And they have a head start on a personality-filled style statement when they move out.

PORTABLE PERSONALITY

WHEN YOU'RE ABOUT TO VENTURE OUT ON YOUR OWN, PLAN AHEAD TO MAKE YOUR NEW DIGS STYLISH AND STREAMLINED. PURCHASE PIECES THAT EASILY WILL MAKE THE TRANSITION WHEREVER YOU LIVE, INTRODUCING COLOR, PERSONALITY, AND INCREASED FUNCTION. JENNIFER AND TALIA'S CABINETS AND SHELVES ARE SMART STORAGE ESSENTIALS FOR ANYONE START-ING OUT. AREA RUGS AND THROW PILLOWS LEND COMFORT AND ZIP TO A NEUTRAL APARTMENT. A FREESTANDING SCREEN ADDS INTEREST AND LETS YOU SPLIT ONE ROOM INTO TWO USES. FINALLY, INVEST IN TABLE AND FLOOR LAMPS TO KEEP YOUR TASKS AND TREASURES IN THE BEST LIGHT.

ABOVE IN A SMALL SHARED ROOM, SKIP THE NIGHTSTANDS AND POSITION A LOW DRESSER BETWEEN THE BEDS. OPPOSITE TALL FREESTANDING CABINETS HELP SEPA-RATE THE LOUNGE AREA FROM THE BEDROOM AREA. A FAUX COWHIDE RUG ADDS PATTERN AND TEXTURE TO THE FLOOR.

DESIGN ESSENTIALS: KIDS' BEDROOMS

Psst ... take a look to see how I create bedrooms that kids love so much, they just might keep them clean!

① ROOM TO GROW

There is nothing wrong with designing a child's room around a theme—say, the circus, the ocean, or a favorite literary character. But if longevity is important to you, take a different tactic. After all, your kid may love teddy bears the first year, then the next year it's the season's most popular cartoon character, then before you know it—the latest rock band.

One way to create a space that grows with your baby is to begin with convertible furnishings, such as a crib that transforms into a twin bed. I also recently found a changing table that offers an open display hutch above and closed storage below. You simply take away the changing pad. Another adaptable option is a desk with drawers and a hutch above. A changing pad can be used on the desktop for the infant stage and then removed as your child grows into a student.

ABOVE A COVERED PAD TRANSFORMS THIS ANTIQUE DRESSER IN KIMBERLY'S NURSERY INTO A CHANGING TABLE. THE PAD IS EASY TO REMOVE WHEN THE DIAPER DAYS ARE DONE. RIGHT IN THE SAME NURSERY, AN IRON BED AWAITS WHEN BABY GROWS INTO A TODDLER. THE BED SKIRT FEATURES LAYERS ADHERED WITH HOOK-AND-LOOP TAPE SO THAT THE LOOK CAN CHANGE INSTANTLY WITHOUT LIFTING THE MATTRESS.

Another quick-change strategy I've used: Create a bed skirt that has three layers of fabric—each layer held in place with hook-and-loop tape. Whenever your child is ready for a new look, tear off a layer. You could have a layer of floral, another of plaid, and another of scalloped lace—all selected to complement a reversible comforter.

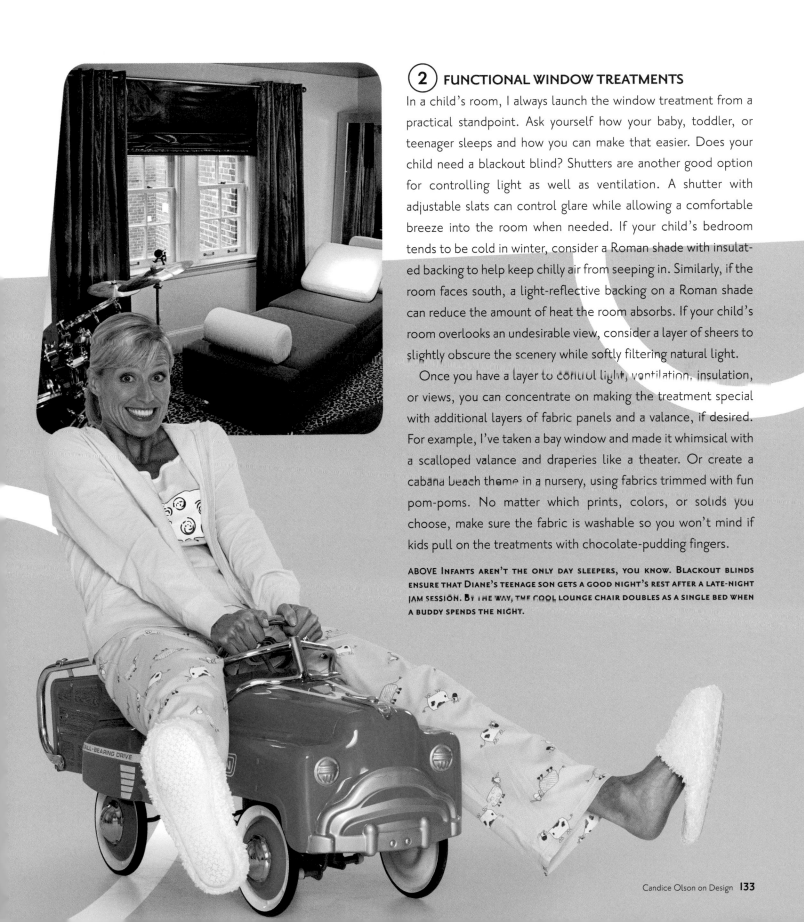

② FUNCTIONAL WINDOW TREATMENTS

In a child's room, I always launch the window treatment from a practical standpoint. Ask yourself how your baby, toddler, or teenager sleeps and how you can make that easier. Does your child need a blackout blind? Shutters are another good option for controlling light as well as ventilation. A shutter with adjustable slats can control glare while allowing a comfortable breeze into the room when needed. If your child's bedroom tends to be cold in winter, consider a Roman shade with insulated backing to help keep chilly air from seeping in. Similarly, if the room faces south, a light-reflective backing on a Roman shade can reduce the amount of heat the room absorbs. If your child's room overlooks an undesirable view, consider a layer of sheers to slightly obscure the scenery while softly filtering natural light.

Once you have a layer to control light, ventilation, insulation, or views, you can concentrate on making the treatment special with additional layers of fabric panels and a valance, if desired. For example, I've taken a bay window and made it whimsical with a scalloped valance and draperies like a theater. Or create a cabana beach theme in a nursery, using fabrics trimmed with fun pom-poms. No matter which prints, colors, or solids you choose, make sure the fabric is washable so you won't mind if kids pull on the treatments with chocolate-pudding fingers.

ABOVE INFANTS AREN'T THE ONLY DAY SLEEPERS, YOU KNOW. BLACKOUT BLINDS ENSURE THAT DIANE'S TEENAGE SON GETS A GOOD NIGHT'S REST AFTER A LATE-NIGHT JAM SESSION. BY THE WAY, THE COOL LOUNGE CHAIR DOUBLES AS A SINGLE BED WHEN A BUDDY SPENDS THE NIGHT.

③ COLOR THEIR WORLD

Wall color is a great place to allow your older children to express their individuality. Bring home a few paint chips and let them pick. Two cans of paint will only set you back $50, so it's easy to change if a color faux pas occurs.

Linens and window treatments are more expensive, so you probably want more control in this arena. Bring home a couple choices in linens and allow your children to select.

Here's a color tip if you have small children: Keep the palette neutral or low contrast because the toys bring in plenty of color.

④ LIGHTS FANTASTIC

In a baby's room, include some kind of fixture that will function as a low-level night-light so that you don't have to flip on all the lights for late-night feedings or changings.

For style that can transition from baby to toddler to teen, try sconces on each side of the bed—on dimmers—so they can function as night-lights and as task lighting.

For any age, you can use recessed fixtures around the perimeter of the room as general illumination and to accent cabinets, highlight artwork, or showcase fabrics.

When your children become teenagers, task lighting becomes particularly important. Include a lamp or wall-mounted light above the study desk. A lamp on the bedside table or mounted on the wall should feature a shade at the correct height so it shields glare from the bulb.

LEFT NOLA'S TEEN DAUGHTER HAD ALREADY PICKED OUT THE GROOVY LINENS TO DRESS THE REFURBISHED IRON BED. I PAIRED THE FABRICS WITH THE BRILLIANT TROPICAL BLUE WALL COLOR. ABOVE IN CAROLINE'S BEDROOM, THE DESKTOP IS FULLY ILLUMINATED IN STYLE WITH THIS FUNKY TRACK-LIGHT FIXTURE.

TIPS OF THE TRADE

THOUGH YOU'LL WANT TO PAINT STORAGE PIECES WITH SCRUBBABLE HIGH-GLOSS LATEX, YOU PROBABLY DON'T WANT THAT SHINY LOOK ON YOUR CHILD'S BEDROOM WALLS. IT'S A SURE THING, HOWEVER, THAT IN A YOUNGER CHILD'S SPACE, THE WALLS WILL TAKE A BATTERING. SO HERE'S A TRICK THAT HELPS YOU AVOID HAVING TO REPAINT AN ENTIRE ROOM FROM TOP TO BOTTOM. INSTALL A CHAIR RAIL 32 TO 36 INCHES ABOVE THE FLOOR. YOU CAN PUT BEADED BOARD OR ANOTHER TYPE OF PANELING BELOW THE RAIL, OR LEAVE IT AS DRYWALL—WHICHEVER SUITS YOUR STYLE—AND PAINT THE LOWER PORTION OF THE WALL A DIFFERENT COLOR THAN THE UPPER SECTION. IF THERE IS AN ACCIDENT, SUCH AS A DRAWING ON THE WALL, YOU ONLY HAVE TO PAINT BELOW THE CHAIR RAIL—UNLESS, OF COURSE, YOUR CHILD IS SOME SORT OF ACROBAT AND MANAGES TO DRAW NEAR THE CEILING!

⑤ STUFF TO STORE

Kids' rooms tend to be smaller spaces, and oh my goodness, have tons of stuff in them. All those itty-bitty red, blue, and yellow plastic things have to go somewhere! You can squeeze additional storage into a modest-size child's bedroom by using multitasking pieces

BEFORE

of furniture, such as an armoire that offers abundant storage for clothing, books, the stereo, television, and a vast collection of CDs and DVDs. Or for an especially tight bedroom space, consider an armoire that opens to reveal a desk for the computer as well as drawers and shelves for textbooks and the trappings of school. As an alternative, construct built-in shelves and cabinets for display and storage.

Whenever you use open shelves, look for attractive baskets or colorful boxes or bins to help corral smaller objects, such as art supplies, papers and pens, jewelry, and CDs.

Another attractive option is to build a long bench beneath a window or along a wall and top it with a cushion for seating—a great place to relax and read or gab with friends. Leave the area below the bench seat open for storage baskets, build in drawers, or design it so that the lid lifts to reveal storage space inside.

To save money on any of your built-in projects, use medium-density fiberboard (MDF) instead of plywood or lumber. You'll need to paint the MDF surfaces with high-gloss, scrubbable latex, but this is a great way to add more color to the room.

ABOVE LEFT AND LEFT To organize all of Nola's teenage daughter's stuff, I positioned a pair of blond open shelves along one wall. The shelves feature storage pieces for stashing CDs, magazines, books, and stereo components. Between the shelves nestles a large storage bench, where friends can sit and junk can hide.

BATHROOMS

SOAK UP SOME OF THESE STYLISH IDEAS FOR CREATING BATHROOMS THAT ARE

EFFICIENT AND CLUTTER-FREE PARADISES FOR PAMPERING.

MODERN SPA

YOU CAN ENJOY A SPA-LIKE ATMOSPHERE IN YOUR BATHROOM—EVEN ONE WITH MODEST DIMENSIONS. THIS ONE PROVES JUST HOW PAMPERED YOU CAN BE.

PINK IS CURRENTLY A POPULAR COLOR BUT ANGELA and Tim understandably weren't crazy about the 1980s peachy-pink fixtures and vanity in their urban bathroom. Plus, with little storage space available, Angela's creams, lotions, and cosmetics cluttered the countertop while poor Tim had nowhere to stash his stuff. Lighting in the bath was so poor that even the light seemed pink.

This couple deserved a romantic spa-like retreat, complete with a tub for two. So we gutted the space and got busy making their home spa dreams come true.

Watery-green glass mosaic wall tiles wrap the room with an air of serenity. For earthy contrast, 12×12-inch slate tiles surface the floor—a selection that won't show dirt.

By borrowing space from an awkward nook that once stood at the end of the old tub, we made room for a longer soaking tub—big enough for two, as requested. A new one-piece toilet further updates the bathroom functions.

BEFORE

With these cool, hard surfaces, the bathroom needed the softening effect and warmth of dark wood. The tub surround, protected by a solid-surface ledge, meets the need. Wood also appears as frames and shelves for dual mirrors and as a base for a custom vanity—the functional focal point for the bath.

A TALL, WALL-MOUNTED CABINET PRESERVES FLOOR SPACE AND PROVIDES ABUNDANT STORAGE. SHALLOW SHELVES MEAN NOTHING GETS LOST AT THE BACK.

OPPOSITE A TALL WOOD CABINET PROVIDES PLENTIFUL SHELVES WHILE BOOSTING THE VISUAL WARMTH OF THE ROOM. RIGHT BLACK FRAMES FOR THE ARTWORK REPEAT THE CHARCOAL TONES OF THE FLOORING. BELOW SURFACING THE WALLS IN WATERY GREEN GLASS TILE CREATES AN ATMOSPHERE OF CALM.

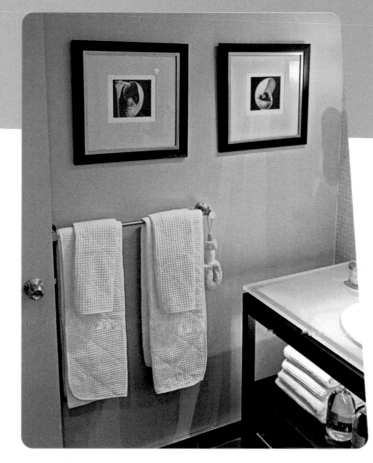

Equipped with three drawers and a large, open shelf below the countertop, the vanity has clean lines and good storage. A translucent blue-green glass top complements the wall mosaics and balances the use of dark wood for the base. Lighted from below, the countertop offers a gorgeous glow that serves as mood lighting for evening soaks and doubles as a night light. A crisp white sink and a sleek, modern chrome faucet and handle—mounted on the wall to keep the countertop clutter-free—finish the vanity with contemporary flair.

Dual mirrors—one above the vanity and the second mounted above the toilet—ensure that Angela and Tim each have a spot for grooming. The dark wood shelf below each can hold

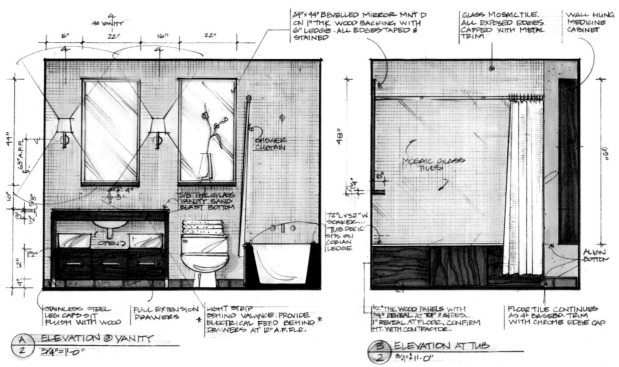

MIRROR

VANITY GLASS COUNTERTOP

WOOD STAIN

PAINT

GLASS WALL TILES

SLATE TILE FLOORING

decorative items, perfumes, a potted plant, or a few attractive jars of cream.

The bulk of the couple's bathroom belongings are stored in a tall, dark-wood cabinet mounted on the wall near the bathroom entry. Though shallow, the cabinet features shelves that are just the right depth for holding loads of cosmetics and toiletries—there is even a shelf available for Tim's stuff!

After appointing the bathroom with terry-cloth and waffle-weave towels and terry-cloth robes, as well as numerous brushes and bottles and jars of bathtime goodies, the couple finally can enjoy the spa life anytime they're home.

SPA SHAPERS

Here are some items to bring into your bathroom to enjoy a spa experience at home:

• Thick, white terry-cloth towels. The fluffier the better.

• White terry-cloth robes. These are wonderful to slip into after a hot shower or a long soak.

• Music. Select mellow tunes to help you relax.

• Candles. Purchase soothing fragrances and light the candles while you bathe.

• Oils, salts, brushes, etc. Pamper yourself with spa products.

ABOVE White waffle-weave cotton towels enhance the spa feel of the bath. Stacked beneath the sink and rolled in a chrome carrier, the towels have a nubby texture that mimics the mosaic tiles visually—and they're invigorating for the skin. OPPOSITE A strip of five-watt halogen bulbs is mounted under the glass countertop to provide lighting from below—a feature that doubles as an easy-on-the-eyes night-light.

SHARED LUXURY

PAMPERING IS DOUBLE THE RELAXING AND TRANQUIL EXPERIENCE IN THIS SPACIOUS BATHROOM BECAUSE IT IS DESIGNED TO BE SHARED BY TWO.

IF YOU'VE EVER DREAMED OF AN INTIMATE RETREAT with a view of the treetops, you might be a little envious of Patricia and Michael's third-floor attic. The couple laid claim to their home's top level, which was once an apartment, to enjoy as their remote and private master suite. But all the architecture that potentially could make the space interesting came off as unfortunately awkward and barely usable. The space, which still contained an odd kitchen and bathroom arrangement, was inefficient and claustrophobic. The uninviting layout drove the couple one level below to invade their sons' bathroom instead. Way too much togetherness!

Ready to reclaim their housetop bedroom and bath, they asked me to make it stylish and functional for two. I set specific goals to make the bathroom both calm and practical and to include perks such as a nicely appointed makeup and vanity area. Storage was another need that I planned to address.

BEFORE

We gutted the space and then produced a soothing, monochromatic setting and unified all the angles, beams, and nooks with a serene coat of cream on the walls and neutral flooring.

The new floor plan features a toilet in its own private alcove and a spacious shower. The separate luxurious oval whirlpool tub

OPPOSITE **The shower fits neatly into a corner but offers a spacious interior with its curving doors.** RIGHT A **partial wall beside the stairwell is just right for this irresistible chaise.** BELOW A **good floor plan lets you envision living in a space before you make changes.**

snuggles up to a gorgeous fireplace—definitely a promisingly romantic addition.

The long, dark-wood vanity provides an ample stretch of countertop and two unusual basin-and-slab sinks so that Patricia and Michael can get ready together. A lower dressing table area beside the vanity allows Patricia a contained spot for applying cosmetics. Opposite the vanity and dressing table is an inviting chaise for spa-like relaxing.

To maintain a relaxing air, clutter needs to go undercover. So I designed a special storage area for the bath. One wall of the

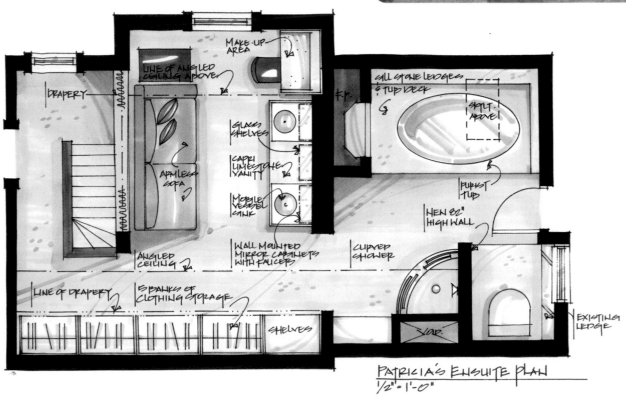

PATRICIA'S ENSUITE PLAN
1/2" = 1'-0"

IN THE BATHROOM, GET ORGANIZED WITH OPEN SHELVES EQUIPPED WITH ATTRACTIVE BASKETS AND BINS SO YOU CAN EASILY SEE AND RETRIEVE WHAT YOU NEED.

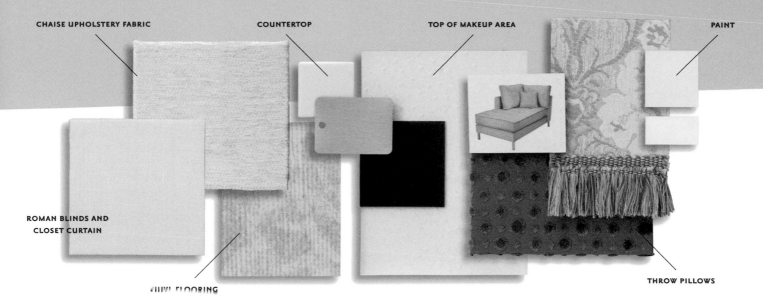

CHAISE

CHAISE UPHOLSTERY FABRIC

COUNTERTOP

TOP OF MAKEUP AREA

PAINT

ROMAN BLINDS AND
CLOSET CURTAIN

VINYL FLOORING

THROW PILLOWS

OPPOSITE IMAGINE LEANING BACK IN THE BATHTUB TO ENJOY STARS FRAMED BY THE
SKYLIGHT AND A CRACKLING FIRE IN THE FIREPLACE. ABOVE FAUCETS INTEGRATED
INTO THE MIRRORS DELIVER STREAMS OF WATER INTO THE BASINS. THE WATER SPILLS
LUXURIOUSLY ONTO THE SLABS BELOW. RIGHT A GIFT FROM THE OCEAN, THIS
GLOWING LIGHT FIXTURE BRINGS TEXTURE AND NATURAL BEAUTY TO THE BATH.

room is given over to storage that is stylishly hidden behind tone-on-tone checkerboard sheers.

I then turned to strategies for brightening this generous bathroom space, which posed some lighting challenges because of the angled ceilings. My solution was to install new insulated recessed lighting and fixtures where space allowed. A track light offers illumination for the tub and features fixtures that can swivel to shine where light is needed most. Just for fun, lighting on the floor creates a runway from the bathroom to the bedroom.

With its new layout and elegant, understated colors and amenities, this third-floor master suite is now a luxurious tree-top retreat.

SMALL WONDER

ISN'T IT NICE TO KNOW THAT DRAMA ISN'T DICTATED BY THE SIZE OF A SPACE? THIS BATHROOM SHOWS HOW A BIG IMPACT CAN COME IN A SMALL PACKAGE.

WENDY'S GUEST BATH IS PROMINENTLY LOCATED at the top of the stairs. Unfortunately it was also unattractive (maybe the inadequate lighting was a good thing). The space was also short on storage and the toilet was kaput. Although the bathroom is small, Wendy wanted it to provide memorable style and to make out-of-town guests feel welcome.

So I booted out the old—a pedestal sink, toilet, bidet, and tub—and set my sights on making this little bath big on beauty and hospitality.

The space formerly filled with the old tub is allotted to a walk-in shower with a frameless glass enclosure that helps make the room appear more spacious. My new palette of elegant ebony, crisp white, and crimson begins with shower walls wrapped in a combination of clean white subway tiles punctuated by a wide band of black and white marble mosaics. White marble mosaics also surface a bench—handy as a spot to sit and

BEFORE

relax to enjoy the steam or shave legs. Black marble mosaics line the shower floor.

To freshen the walls and create unity with the white shower tiles, I chose clean white for the bathroom walls. Elegant, textural, black slate tiles on the floor balance the use of white.

A FRAMELESS GLASS SHOWER ENCLOSURE CREATES THE ILLUSION OF A LARGER BATHROOM SPACE.

A functional, beautiful vanity replaces the pedestal sink. For this piece, tall mirrors crown an ebony-stained oak shelf, which serves as a dramatic backdrop for the marble mosaic countertop. Open shelving below provides conveniently accessible storage. Without question, the most memorable element in the bathroom is the red glass vessel-style sink, which rests on the mosaic countertop like an elegant serving bowl. A sleek wall-mounted faucet and handles preserve counter space.

Of course, I couldn't leave these beautiful features in the dark, so I added the right lighting, including a waterproof shower fixture, recessed ceiling spots, undercabinet lighting in the storage unit, and sconces mounted on the vanity mirror.

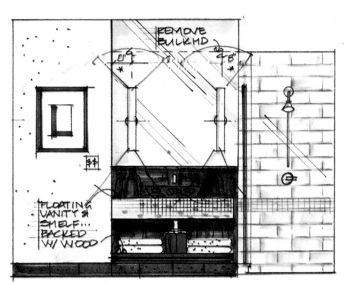

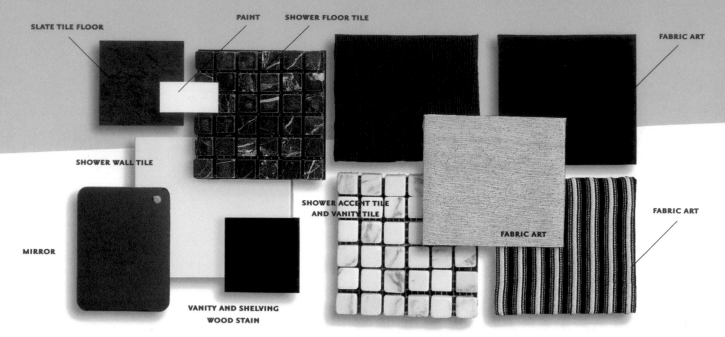

SLATE TILE FLOOR

PAINT SHOWER FLOOR TILE

FABRIC ART

SHOWER WALL TILE

MIRROR

SHOWER ACCENT TILE
AND VANITY TILE

FABRIC ART

FABRIC ART

VANITY AND SHELVING
WOOD STAIN

To continue Wendy's use of art throughout her home, I wanted a creative addition in the bathroom that would stand up to the humidity. A fabric tapestry—hung to the left of the doorway (not visible in the photos)—augments my color scheme and introduces an appealing composition of geometric shapes. Above the toilet, an arrangement of four red decorative tiles adds more artful interest. Other finishing touches include a basket of toiletries in the shower, several red accent pieces, and towels and soaps. Now this bright, contemporary bathroom is ready to welcome and pamper guests for years to come. However, it is so nice that Wendy may even decide to use it herself!

VESSEL BASINS

IF YOU DECIDE TO PURCHASE A VESSEL SINK, WHICH LOOKS LIKE A BOWL SITTING ON THE COUNTERTOP, KEEP THESE CONSIDERATIONS IN MIND:
• ADJUST THE HEIGHT OF THE COUNTERTOP SO THE BASIN WILL REST AT A COMFORTABLE HEIGHT.
• PAIR THE SINK WITH A TALL, GOOSENECK FAUCET OR ONE THAT MOUNTS IN THE WALL ABOVE. THIS WILL MEAN PLUMBING MUST BE INSTALLED BEFORE DRYWALLING. A FAUCET INSTALLED TOO HIGH CAN YIELD SPLASHES.
• A VESSEL SINK CAN BE A GOOD CHOICE FOR A GUEST BATH, BUT IN A BATH RECEIVING LOTS OF USE, A GLASS OR POTTERY VESSEL SINK COULD CHIP OR CRACK IF SOMETHING AS SMALL AS A PERFUME BOTTLE IS DROPPED ON IT.

ABOVE AN ADJUSTABLE SHOWERHEAD ACCOMMODATES GUESTS OF DIFFERENT HEIGHTS. OPPOSITE EBONY STAINED OAK AND A MOSAIC TILED COUNTERTOP ARE REPEATED IN THE STORAGE AREA OPPOSITE THE VANITY. THE SLATE FLOORING AND MARBLE MOSAICS LAVISH THE BATH IN TEXTURE.

MOM AND DAD'S OASIS

ELEGANTLY EMBOSSED WALLS, LIMESTONE AND MARBLE FLOORING, AND POSH PAMPERING AMENITIES MAKE THIS AN ADULTS-ONLY RETREAT.

IT'S UNDERSTANDABLE THAT KIDS LOVE MOM AND Dad's bathroom, and Phil and Jayne's children were no exception. It wasn't long before the couple's old master bathroom began showing signs of the creative nature these young ones possessed. Carpeting was "decorated" with stains, and interesting wall designs were innovatively formed by peeling off wallpaper with little fingers. Toys even crammed an unused bidet!

It's no wonder Phil and Jayne finally were ready to reclaim this space as their own. The couple already had dreamed up some must-haves, including a generously sized soaking tub for Jayne. Phil simply wanted to say goodbye to the toy box bidet.

To make way for the luxuries I had in mind, some of the fixtures needed to be relocated. The tub, for example, shifted into the corner once occupied by the bidet. This left a space for installing a large luxury walk-in shower. Removing the radiator

and moving the toilet under the window made room for a long double-sink vanity equipped with a makeup counter for Jayne.

When choosing a color palette for the new bathroom, I drew inspiration from the adjoining master bedroom. Repeating the bedroom's neutral scheme in the limestone floor tiles, marble inlay, and the wall finish turns the master bath and bedroom into a cohesive suite.

To give the bathroom its own personality, I specified an unusual wall finish that offers the look of elegantly flocked wallcovering. But it is actually stenciled plaster designs glazed with a beautiful gold finish.

To show off this beautifully patterned and dimensional surface, I lit the bath with a chandelier over the tub and sconces above the vanity. A waterproof recessed fixture brightens the shower. Natural light is available through the bath's lone window, which I made more grand with a valance installed at ceiling height.

OPEN UNDER.

JUMBLED MARBLE INSERT

B

BUILT-IN BENCH

36"X 72" SOAKER TUB

SOLID SURFACE COUNTER FROM WALL TO DOOR FRAME

REPOSITIONED TOILET UNDER WINDOW

OPPOSITE A FRAMELESS GLASS ENCLOSURE PUTS THE BEAUTIFUL LIMESTONE AND MARBLE MOSAICS IN THE SHOWER ON DISPLAY. ABOVE A STAND AT ONE END OF THE BATH CRADLES OODLES OF TOWELS. LEFT AN INEFFICIENT FLOOR PLAN ISN'T WORTH PRESERVING TO SAVE MONEY. IN THIS CASE, RELOCATING FIXTURES WAS NECESSARY TO MAKE THE BATHROOM FUNCTIONAL.

MAXIMIZE YOUR BATHING OPTIONS BY INCLUDING A GENEROUS SHOWER ENCLOSURE AS WELL AS A SEPARATE SOAKER TUB.

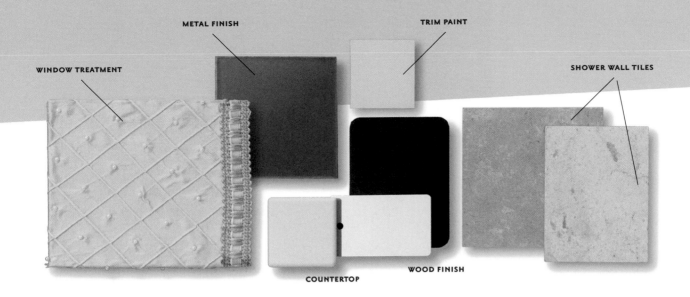

WINDOW TREATMENT

METAL FINISH

TRIM PAINT

SHOWER WALL TILES

COUNTERTOP

WOOD FINISH

On the floor, classic limestone tiles frame an inlay of irregular-shape tumbled marble. An in-floor heating system replaced the need for the old radiator, so we could use that under-the-window space for the toilet.

The long vanity is equipped with dual sinks and storage below to accommodate Phil and Jayne as well as their bathroom-related belongings.

Now, the toys are tucked away elsewhere in the house and the pampering amenities and elegant surfaces and finishes clearly signal that this is a space just for Mom and Dad.

WOW! WALLS

FOR THE WALL TREATMENT, WE STARTED BY INSTALLING TRADITIONAL PANELED WAINSCOTING ON THE LOWER HALF OF THE WALLS; WE PAINTED IT WHITE. (THE WAINSCOTING EFFECT REPEATS AROUND THE TUB FOR CONTINUITY.) UPPER WALLS WERE ROLLED WITH A COAT OF GOLD PAINT AND ALLOWED TO DRY. METALLIC GLAZE THEN COVERED THE PAINT AND WAS TOPPED WITH VENETIAN PLASTER, WHICH WAS APPLIED THROUGH A STENCIL TO CREATE A LUXURIOUS EMBOSSED FINISH.

ABOVE GLASS LIDDED JARS TURN EVERYDAY NECESSITIES INTO OBJECTS OF BEAUTY. OPPOSITE DARK WOOD AND A CLEAN WHITE SOLID-SURFACE COUNTERTOP COMBINE WITH CHROME FAUCETS AND FITTINGS FOR A LOOK THAT HINTS AT VINTAGE ROOTS BUT FEELS MODERN. SILVER MIRROR FRAMES REPEAT THE METALLIC COLOR.

DESIGN ESSENTIALS: BATHROOMS

EVERYTHING'S DUCKY IN A BATHROOM THAT'S DESIGNED
WITH THESE BASIC PRINCIPLES IN MIND.

① A CLEAN START

Although most bathrooms are small, averaging about 7X10 feet, they can take a big bite out of your remodeling and decorating budget. That's why I try to choose permanent elements that promise longevity. Choose components and surfaces that are neutral but not necessarily monochromatic. Let the accessories and art make your artistic statements.

You also can make your small bath live large by keeping it clutterfree with well-planned storage. A floor-to-ceiling cabinet on one wall can be only 5 to 6 inches deep and store an abundance of toiletries and bathroom cleaning supplies. To keep your countertops clear, consider deep drawers for storing bulky items such as the hair dryer or electric curlers. If you have the space, design your bathroom with a countertop appliance garage (much like you would find in a

BEFORE

kitchen); include outlets at the back of the storage compartment so your appliances can stay plugged in.

Because loads of fluffy white towels make a bathroom seem more luxurious, consider keeping stacks on display on open shelves or on a chair beside the bathtub. Don't forget a hook for hanging your white terry-cloth robe!

RIGHT OPEN SHELVING BELOW THE TWIN SINKS KEEPS TOWELS AND TOILETRIES IN EASY REACH, BUT TO AVOID A CLUTTERED LOOK, IT'S IMPORTANT TO KEEP ITEMS TIDILY ARRANGED.

If you love wood, bamboo is a wonderful choice for the bathroom because it handles the high humidity gracefully. I've even used it on a bathroom ceiling as an intimate canopy over a tub. Alternatively, wood-look laminate flooring can be used in a bathroom, but it must be specially installed to prevent water from seeping into its sublayer.

As with flooring, stone countertops look beautiful in the bathroom too. But keep in mind that—just as in the kitchen—more porous stones, such as marble and limestone, will stain. Consider stone with a polished surface because it is easier to clean. Also, today's manufactured "stones" are terrific alternatives and offer plenty of design flexibility because you can use them to surface a shower or the tub deck.

For more interest, you can combine materials. On the floor, create a border using one stone and a center design using another type of stone or tile. This variety can reappear on walls too. I once lined a shower with solid-surface material inset with a bit of tile.

② ON THE SURFACE

We are doing more and more bathrooms with modern, clean, pared-down lines. But with so many hard surfaces in a bath, I try to include some natural elements as a foil for the synthetic components, such as the porcelain. That's one reason I love

natural stone and wood: Pair those with the sparkle of a mirror and chrome faucets and hardware, and you have something special.

If you're considering a stone floor, select a non-slip finish or choose a stone with a surface that is naturally textured and unpolished, such as slate or limestone, so your feet easily grip the surface even when it is wet. Another option that is beautiful and safe is smooth stone cut into smaller tiles (4×4, 6×6, or 8×8 inches). This is more slip-resistant than large tiles thanks to the increased number of grout seams.

3 SIZZLING ACCESSORIES

I'm not a big fan of colored towels for spicing up the bath, but I love to mix in something a little out of the ordinary—a Buddha sculpture, for example. I also like to use things that connect the bath to outdoor elements, such as the beach, by including a container of shells or sea sponges. Artwork is a good way to bring color into the bathroom too. If you do bring in artwork, don't use anything expensive as the high humidity eventually could damage the piece. Or try using artwork impervious to moisture, such as ceramic tile or fabric.

BEFORE

4 LUXURIES GALORE

There's no shortage of amenities you can introduce into your bathroom for pampering yourself to your heart's content.

Big bathtubs seem to top everyone's list. Before you buy, climb into the one you're considering—clothes on, of course!—to see if it is deep enough and comfortable.

Spacious showers equipped with multiple showerheads and body sprays are a wonderfully relaxing addition to the bath. Some showers (and tubs) include fiber-optic lighting with changing light colors to influence your mood. See "Shopping Tip," opposite, to learn ways to view the variety of tubs, showers, faucets, and showerheads available.

So that you stay toasty on cold days, consider an in-floor heating system that warms the tiles or stone you walk on. Racks that heat your towels also are available. Finish your bath with a cushy lounge chair or a soft sofa.

ABOVE FOR THE ULTIMATE IN DECADENT LUXURY, LOOK INTO TUB FILLERS THAT POUR WATER IN A STREAM FROM THE CEILING. LEFT LOOK AROUND YOUR HOUSE OR SHOP GARDEN CENTERS TO FIND WATERPROOF OR WATER-TOLERANT STATUES THAT ARE JUST RIGHT FOR ACCENTING A TUB SURROUND OR VANITY COUNTERTOP.

SHOPPING TIP

IF YOU LIVE NEAR A LARGE CITY, CHECK OUT THE KITCHEN AND BATH SHOWROOMS THAT MAKE SHOPPING FOR TUBS, FAUCETS, SHOWERS, AND SHOWERHEADS A SENSATIONAL EXPERIENCE. YOU'LL FIND WONDERFUL DISPLAYS FEATURING LINES OF FUNCTIONING TUBS AND SHOWERS WITH VALUABLE INFORMATION. FOR EXAMPLE, PEOPLE LOVE BIG RAIN SHOWERHEADS, BUT SOMETIMES WHEN THEY REALIZE THEY OFFER NO ADJUSTABILITY OR THAT THEY DON'T MAKE THE SHOWER EASIER TO CLEAN, THEY DECIDE ON SOMETHING ELSE.

HERE'S ANOTHER THING TO COMPARE: ONE OF THE DRAWBACKS TO WHIRLPOOL TUBS IS THAT YOU CAN'T USE THOSE GORGEOUS SCENTED OILS AND BUBBLES. AIR TUBS, ON THE OTHER HAND, CAN HANDLE THESE GOODIES. THEY USE AIR TO GENTLY "BUBBLE" THE WATER AND OPERATE MORE QUIETLY THAN A WHIRLPOOL.

⑤ LIGHTING TO LOVE

When positioning lighting in a bathroom, give every fixture purpose. After all, what's the purpose in lighting air? Recessed fixtures with adjustable lenses will let you angle and direct the beam of light to a vertical piece of cabinetry or artwork.

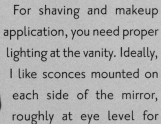

For shaving and makeup application, you need proper lighting at the vanity. Ideally, I like sconces mounted on each side of the mirror, roughly at eye level for even illumination. Add a frosted shade so there is no harsh glare. I am not a fan of a row of small makeup lights across the top of the mirror (see the Before photo above). But if that's the fixture you have, substitute the clear bulbs for frosted, and you'll make an improvement in the quality of the light.

Other lighting concerns to keep in mind include having a light inside the shower so you're not showering in the shadows. Likewise, position recessed fixtures (or even a chandelier) above the bathtub.

Have your lights installed on dimmers. You'll want medium-to-high lighting levels when you get ready in the morning and when you are cleaning the bathroom. But when it is time to wind down in the evening and take a long, relaxing soak in the tub, you'll want low-light levels. Don't forget the candles!

ABOVE LEFT IN SCOTT AND KELLY'S MASTER BATHROOM, SCONCES FLANK THE MIRROR TO LIGHT EACH SIDE OF THE FACE. RECESSED HALOGEN LIGHTS BOOST OVERALL LIGHTING BUT ALSO CAST LIGHT ON THE COUNTERTOP; THE OTHER RECESSED FIXTURE SPOTLIGHTS A SCULPTURE.

BASEMENTS

One of the greatest things about basements is that they can serve any function that fits your needs. Entertain these lower-level living ideas.

DOWN-UNDER DELIGHT

LET THIS BASEMENT MAKEOVER INSPIRE YOU TO SOLVE COMMON BASEMENT PROBLEMS WITH STYLISH SOLUTIONS.

WALLPAPER IS ONE OF THOSE DECORATIVE ELEMENTS that can be a blessing or a curse. When it's new and you've chosen the pattern wisely, it can lend style to your space. But in the case of Holly and David's basement, an overzealous allotment of plaid wallpaper was definitely too much of a good thing. They were so put off by the paper that they rarely ventured "down under."

I came in to make sure that all that great space wouldn't go to waste, formulating a new look and layout that would be as welcoming for Mom and Dad as it would be for kids.

Peeling off the wallpaper revealed yet another visual offender—old wood paneling. To bring an air of tranquillity to the basement (a far cry from all that high-contrast, busy plaid), I chose a soft mushroom hue for the walls. We also waved goodbye to the eye-popping raspberry-color carpet and welcomed a neutral carpeting that's a darker shade than the walls. The carpeting stops short of one end of the room where I

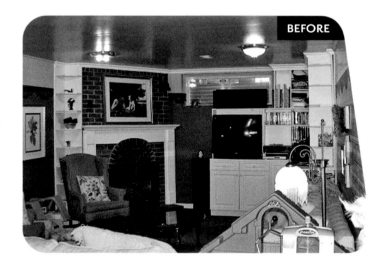

reserved one-quarter of the space for kids. For this area, wood-tone laminate flooring complements the carpeting and serves as a practical, easy-to-clean option. Using warm, understated color on the walls and floor gives the room a cozy, calm feel and makes the space seem larger.

IF YOU HAVE ONE OF THESE QUIRKY CORNER FIREPLACES, TRY ANGLING YOUR FURNITURE IN THE SAME MANNER. THE SPACE WILL FEEL MORE BALANCED AND ANCHORED.

OPPOSITE MUSHROOM TONES WRAP THE BASEMENT WALLS, FLOOR, AND EVEN THE FIREPLACE IN CALMING, LOW-CONTRAST COLOR. RIGHT THIS PAINTED CABINET AND MIRROR LEND CASUAL CHARACTER AND A SPLASH OF SUBTLE COLOR TO THE ROOM. BELOW ONE WELL-PLANNED BUILT-IN PROVIDES STORAGE, DISPLAY, AND SEATING.

Plush chenille curtain panels—hung on a rod that stretches across the width of the basement where flooring materials meet—can pull closed to hide toys on the kids' side. The "soft wall" also provides privacy for overnight guests using the new sleeper sofa.

In addition to redesigning the basement so it functions as a guest room and as a playroom, the space also can serve as a great spot for entertaining and television viewing. To provide a platform for the television and to create additional seating and storage, I designed a custom built-in bench to replace old cabinetry beside the fireplace.

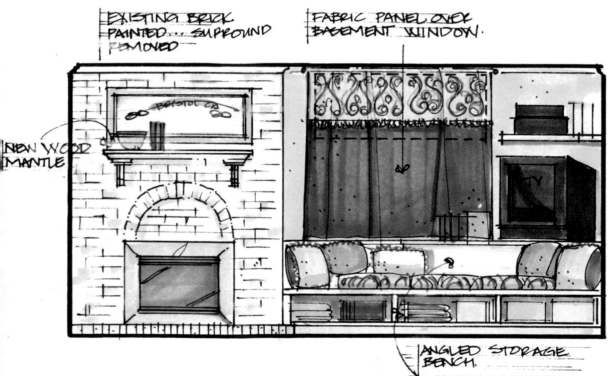

EXISTING BRICK PAINTED...SURROUND REMOVED

FABRIC PANEL OVER BASEMENT WINDOW.

NEW WOOD MANTLE

ANGLED STORAGE BENCH.

PAINT

SOFA UPHOLSTERY

DRAPERIES

FLOORING

DRAPERIES

The fireplace was another eyesore that had to be dealt with. Its odd angle and poorly crafted brick face were definitely unappealing. Although the couple originally wanted a whole new fireplace, I thought the budget would be better spent on new lighting. (The ceiling-mounted fixtures made the low basement ceiling positively oppressive!) So instead, I freshened the fireplace with paint, a new mantel, and a screen to obscure the dirty firebox interior.

The money saved on the fireplace was invested in new recessed fixtures, which don't draw attention to themselves or gobble up headroom. Instead, the adjustable fixtures are directed to put the spotlight on the textures and hues of the artwork, the built-in bench, and the curtain panels (chenille panels to match the "soft dividing wall" are hung over the small basement window too).

The resulting combination of new fabrics, furnishings, paint, and lighting have completely erased the memory of all that plaid wallpaper. Now the family and their friends can't wait to make a visit "down under."

ABOVE THE FORMER SURROUND DIDN'T SEEM TO FIT THE FIREPLACE FACADE. THIS MANTEL, WHICH IS PAINTED TO MATCH THE BRICKS, KEEPS THIS FOCAL POINT SIMPLE YET ELEGANT. OPPOSITE PLUSH CHENILLE CURTAINS HANG FROM A CEILING-MOUNTED DRAPERY ROD; WHEN DESIRED, THEY DRAW TO HIDE THE KIDS' PLAY AREA.

FAMILY CLUBHOUSE

FAMILY, FRIENDS, AND STUDENTS OF THE HOMEOWNERS CAN ENJOY THIS BASEMENT SPACE, WHERE THERE'S SOMETHING FOR EVERYONE.

FOR TENNIS PRO NICHOLAS AND HIS WIFE, DEBBIE, this home's large backyard, tennis court, swimming pool, and spacious walkout basement—complete with wet bar and fireplace—were tremendous selling points that persuaded them to buy. But the basement family room's 1970s decor of orange-yellow carpeting, wood paneling, and lime-striped wallpaper was no "match" for them. So I came onto the court to serve up a look and layout to suit their needs. Nicholas wanted the family room to be a place where his students could relax after tennis lessons; Debbie laid claim to the other end of the basement, requesting that it accommodate family television viewing, game playing, and conversing beside the fireplace.

I sent the outdated features out the door and strengthened the room's connection to the outdoors with colors reminiscent of sandy beaches, blue water, and fresh tennis whites. For more zip, I mixed in shining chrome accents.

BEFORE

This space was long and large enough to handle more than one wall color, so I freshened adjacent walls with ocean blue and sandy gold. Blue-gray broadloom carpet gives the space an infinitely more elegant look than that old orange rug! Brickwork around the fireplace and the existing cabinetry in the family area

are reborn with a fresh coat of white paint. Blue ultrasuede fabric renews the bar front.

A few things increase the style and function of the basement: Enlarging the existing cabinetry, for example, makes it deep enough to accommodate the TV. Behind the bar, a modern wood panel detail is mounted on the wall. A similar element links the fireplace to the bar.

Next, we replaced the old light fixtures with new halogen track lighting. These fixtures can be directed at furniture, artwork, or other key points. Decorative sconces fit into the new wood detailing over the bar and fireplace.

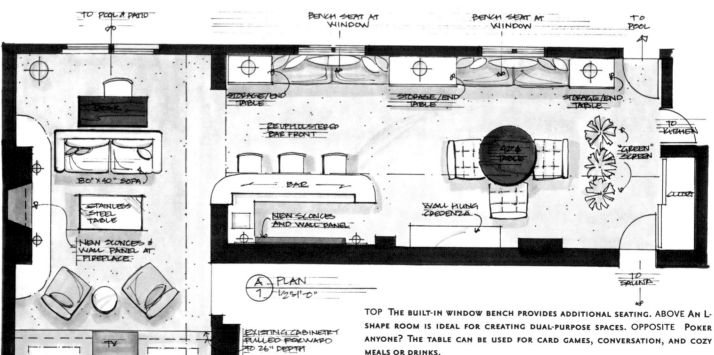

TOP THE BUILT-IN WINDOW BENCH PROVIDES ADDITIONAL SEATING. ABOVE AN L-SHAPE ROOM IS IDEAL FOR CREATING DUAL-PURPOSE SPACES. OPPOSITE POKER ANYONE? THE TABLE CAN BE USED FOR CARD GAMES, CONVERSATION, AND COZY MEALS OR DRINKS.

HALOGEN TRACK-LIGHTING FIXTURES PROVIDE MARVELOUS PINPOINT LIGHTING FOR A BASEMENT. THE INDIVIDUAL FIXTURES EASILY CAN BE DIRECTED TOWARD A FOCAL POINT, SUCH AS ART OR THE FIREPLACE.

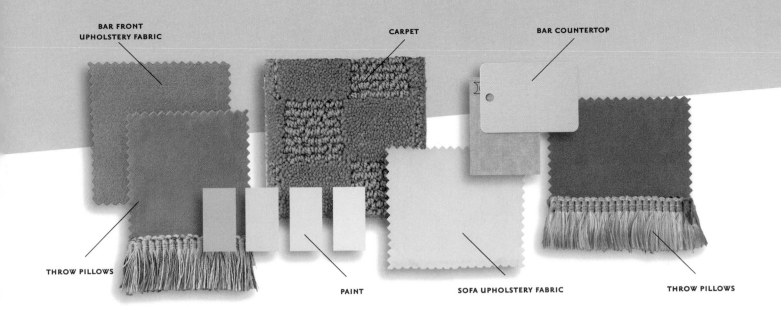

BAR FRONT
UPHOLSTERY FABRIC

CARPET

BAR COUNTERTOP

THROW PILLOWS

PAINT

SOFA UPHOLSTERY FABRIC

THROW PILLOWS

With the background details in place, I turned my attention to the furnishings. A comfy white sofa, a clean-lined coffee table, and a pair of streamlined slipper chairs form an inviting area for conversation in front of the fireplace. The slipper chairs won't block the view to the TV.

Opposite the bar, built-in storage tables and benches line the wall to increase the function and entertainment value of the space. Because this end of the family room is also where bathers come inside from the swimming pool, I added a wooden screen and some greenery to create a private "corridor" to adjacent spaces.

With these finishing touches in place, the "clubhouse" is open for business. The space is definitely a match made in heaven for Nicholas and Debbie—not to mention family, friends, and students.

RIGHT **The bar end of the basement accommodates tennis students, while the near end welcomes family and friends. OPPOSITE Tufted, durable faux suede provides a soft, cushiony finish for the base of the bar, which was once dressed in orange vinyl. The plush upholstered treatment plays a key role in giving the basement a luxurious feel.**

PEACE AND PLAY

HIGH-STYLE PARENTS AND ACTIVE KIDS CAN COHABIT THIS BASEMENT, EQUIPPED WITH AREAS FOR ADULT CONVERSATION AND YOUNGSTER PLAYTIME.

CLUTTER CAN CAUSE A MINIMALIST TO REVOLT, so it wasn't surprising that Adele and Brian longed to bring order to their lower-level family room. This couple appreciates sleek, streamlined styling and the rest of their 1970s home—which they had carefully renovated—reflected their well-refined tastes. Downstairs, however, was more of a natural reflection of the couple's two young daughters, where chaos—rather than calm—was currently king. I stepped in to overthrow the ruling mob of toys and art supplies and vowed to bring serenity to the land. This meant creating clear boundaries for adults versus kids.

Although Adele and Brian hadn't employed very much color upstairs, I started by giving the fireplace a makeover using mosaic tiles of iridescent creams, purples, greens, blues, and browns. The muted tones are calming and work in tandem with the clean, open feeling established upstairs.

BEFORE

The colors continue to fabric panels, which I added to define the two basement areas—a contemporary conversation zone in front of the fireplace for Mom, Dad, and friends and a play area for the kids. Flooring materials change from area to area as well: carpet for adults and low-maintenance vinyl for the kids.

SELECT EASY-CARE FLOORING AND DURABLE WORK SURFACES FOR KIDS' PLAY AREAS. TASK LIGHTING KEEPS PROJECTS ON TRACK, AND AMPLE STORAGE BINS (AS WELL AS DIVIDING CURTAINS) MAINTAIN TIDINESS.

OPPOSITE For continuity, fabrics used for the kids' room divider reappear as window treatments in the adult zone. The sink in the kids' area is out of view at the end of the counter. RIGHT The oversize silver "flower" is a chair. BELOW Lots of shelves maintain order for the family room.

The walls are painted in a durable, washable latex that can stand up to sticky fingers, but the soft cream color is soothing and delicate in appearance. Repeating the sheen and shading of the walls are the fabrics used for the room divider as well as for panels at the patio door.

To furnish the adult area in style, I brought in a smoky, steel-blue sectional sofa (upholstered in easy-care faux suede), an amoeba-shape midcentury-modern glass coffee table, and a playful, silver, flowerlike chair.

Augmenting the newly refaced fireplace is a wood mantel. It bridges the gap between custom-built shelves designed to hold the television and its accompanying media equipment as well as a variety of decorative objects.

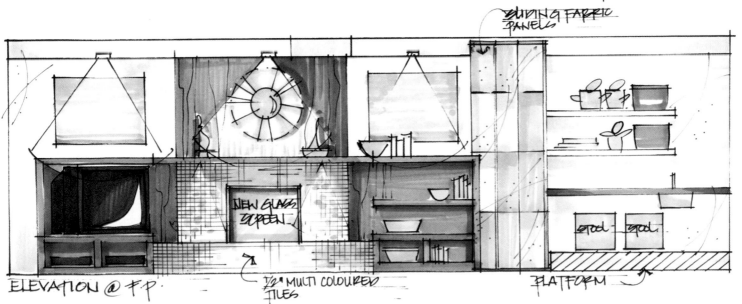

ELEVATION @ F.P.   1/2" MULTI COLOURED TILES   PLATFORM

SLIDING FABRIC PANELS

NEW GLASS SCREEN

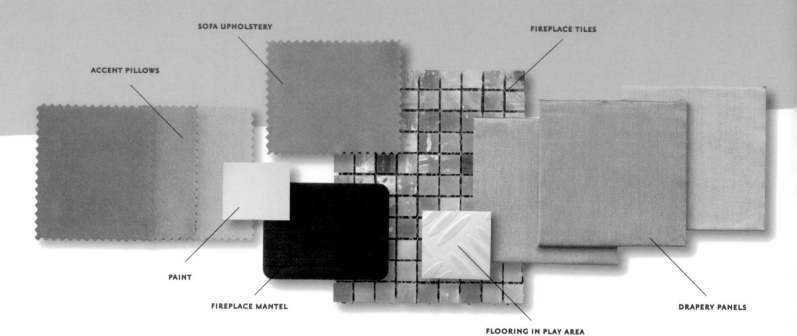

ACCENT PILLOWS

SOFA UPHOLSTERY

FIREPLACE TILES

PAINT

FIREPLACE MANTEL

FLOORING IN PLAY AREA

DRAPERY PANELS

Because even a walkout basement can seem dark, adequate lighting was important to really make this new space as beautiful as it could be. To show off the mosaic kaleidoscope on the fireplace, I specified two lights under the mantel. A gracefully arching stainless-steel floor lamp reaches out into the center of the room. For the kids, lights mounted beneath their storage shelves illuminate the work surface below.

Order now reigns in this subterranean kingdom, and both kids and adults can enjoy the benefits of living in a clean and stylish setting.

ABOVE COLORS THROUGHOUT THE BASEMENT FAMILY ROOM—INCLUDING THE HUES OF THESE ACCENT PIECES—ARE INSPIRED BY THE FIREPLACE MOSAIC TILES. OPPOSITE A BOOMERANG-SHAPE COFFEE TABLE INTRODUCES A CASUAL RETRO ELEMENT TO THE CONVERSATION AREA.

DESIGN ESSENTIALS: BASEMENTS

LOWER-LEVEL SPACES CAN BE AS STYLISH AND USEFUL AS ANY UPPER-LEVEL ROOMS. HERE'S HOW TO BRING DRAMA DOWN UNDER.

① CLEAR THE CLUTTER

Basements often become the catchall for everything you can't find a place for upstairs. It's a case of "out of sight, out of mind," and this subterranean treasure turns into a bunker for bikes, junk, and the kitty litter. In essence, you have an ugly-duckling space, and you want to end up with a swan.

So how do you get rid of all the clutter? Truthfully, I've found most people want to hang on to a lot of it. But I suggest starting with a checklist; use it to decide what you want to keep and what you can give away that someone else could use. The rest has to go to the curb. With whatever remains, the key is to organize, contain, and hide the ugly stuff.

If you don't have a room in your basement that will be designated for storage only, take stock of everything you have to store and make a place for it.

ABOVE PAULA'S BASEMENT WAS LIKE MANY—LOTS OF STUFF! RIGHT IT WAS ALSO QUITE SMALL, SO I DECIDED TO TUCK STORAGE SHELVES BEHIND MOVABLE WALLS. CAN'T SEE THE DOORS? THEY'RE BEHIND THE ARTWORK ON THE LEFT.

If your basement is especially small, you have to look for creative solutions, such as hiding shelves behind movable walls as I did in the basement shown below and opposite. Other options include building in cabinetry or adding open shelves that can hold decorative storage bins. You also can use pieces that double for storage, such as a storage bench or ottoman.

② MAKE IT MULTIPURPOSE

You may "want it all" in the basement—meaning you need it to function as a guest room, a playroom, an adult recreation zone, a place for watching television or reading or playing pool—well, you get the idea. Whew!

As in a combined living room and dining room, you can use furniture groupings to define zones for specific activities. Furniture with multiple functions can help you increase the usefulness of the basement as well. For a play space that doubles as a guest room, purchase a sleeper sofa, a futon, or a daybed that looks like a sofa. A daybed with a trundle below can convert to a guest bed for two. Just throw off the decorative pillows at night and pull out the trundle.

If you want an area for the kids, include a desktop for doing crafts and homework and select easy-care finishes and flooring (see "Flooring Factors" on page 188). You also might consider creating a visual barrier between you and the kids by hanging soft fabric panel "walls" or using a freestanding screen or two.

If you want to play pool in the basement, you need an area large enough for the size of the pool table as well as for using the long pool cues. Any good pool table dealer can provide you with the optimum room measurements for the table you have in mind.

Other nice features for a multipurpose basement include a second kitchen with cabinetry, a countertop, a small sink, a microwave oven for popping popcorn (for movies) and an undercounter refrigerator for beverages. Add a half-bath to the basement, and you might not want to go back upstairs!

ABOVE LEFT SLIDING DOORS OPEN TO REVEAL AN ABUNDANCE OF SHELVES FOR STOWING BEDDING FOR A FOLDOUT SOFA AS WELL AS A SPOT FOR THE TELEVISION. THIS MAKES UP FOR THE LACK OF SPACE FOR AN ENTERTAINMENT ARMOIRE.

③ SUBTLE CEILINGS

In addition to using lighting creatively to pull attention away from the ceiling (see "Tricks of Light" opposite), you can use paint to downplay less-appealing architecture. Keep your color palette neutral or low-contrast and wrap the room—the walls, the ceiling, and even the flooring—in the same tones for a seamless look that visually expands space.

If you're "blessed" with the old style of dropped ceiling and don't want to replace it, you can paint the tiles and metal framework; prime everything first, let dry, and spray paint for a fast finish.

④ FLOORING FACTORS

You also can use changes in flooring materials to define different zones in the basement. In the adult area, you could use carpeting, which is popular for basement rooms because it is warm under foot. Make this subterranean space seem even cozier by layering a deep-pile area rug over the carpeting.

If you decide on wood flooring, make sure it is suitable for below-grade application (ask the flooring dealer) because if humidity is seeping in, the floor will warp. (See "Start Smart" opposite.)

In the kids' zone, choose stain-resistant, easy-clean flooring such as sheet vinyl or laminate. That way, kids can work on messy projects and you won't flip your lid.

ABOVE WARM YELLOW BROADLOOM CARPETING IN SARAH'S GATHERING AREA GIVES WAY TO EASY-CARE, TOUGH SHEET-VINYL FLOORING IN THE ARTS AND CRAFTS ZONE. ABOVE LEFT EXPOSED PIPES AND BUSY CARPETING MAKE THE BASEMENT UNAPPEALING. LEFT PAINTING THE EXPOSED PIPES AND CEILING THE SAME COLOR ALLOWS THE UNATTRACTIVE FEATURES TO SEEM LESS INTRUSIVE.

START SMART

It generally costs as much to finish a lower-level living space as it does upper-level areas. You don't want your money to go down the drain because dampness has ruined your redo!

If your basement has moisture problems, there are a few simple tactics you can try before calling in the waterproofing pros. First, make sure that your gutters and downspouts are clear of debris. Second, the earth around the house should gently slope away from the foundation. If the soil tilts toward the house, try adding a few inches of dirt to create the necessary downgrade. After that, consider having a sump pump installed to carry subterranean water away from the house.

If these strategies fail, you may need to call in a contractor to look at other waterproofing options.

If your basement ceiling is especially low and you're desperate for more living space, you may want to have the basement dug deeper to create more headroom.

⑤ TRICKS OF LIGHT

The ceiling often is lower in the basement than in other parts of the house, so recessed fixtures are a good choice here because they won't interfere with headroom. Position the fixtures around the perimeter of the room to visually push out the walls and make the space appear to expand.

You also can use wall washers (adjustable recessed fixtures) to throw light down a wall to highlight a textured finish, draw attention to a fireplace, show off the fabric of a window treatment, or spotlight artwork. Typically, the light should be 16 to 18 inches from the wall so it can rake down the vertical surfaces.

To eliminate shadowy corners, position an accent light on the floor to shine light upward on a plant, sculpture, or even a vase on a pedestal. You also can position an accent light on a shelf for a moody effect.

If your lighting budget is limited, you can use track lights in a low-ceiling basement—just make sure the tracks are positioned close to the wall so that people won't bump their heads on the dropped fixtures.

Because basements without walkouts typically feature small 18-inch-tall windows, the availability of natural light can become a special concern. Rather than fight the fact, I'll sometimes use full-height draperies to treat a small window, creating the illusion of a larger window.

ABOVE LEFT RECESSED LIGHTING—EVEN IN THIS WINDOW WELL—ILLUMINATES PAULA'S DARK BASEMENT BECAUSE THESE FIXTURES DON'T TAKE UP HEADROOM. I ALSO MADE THIS SMALL WINDOW AT THE END OF THE ROOM APPEAR LARGER AND BRIGHTER BY ADDING MIRRORS ON EACH SIDE.

INDEX